LIVING OR DEAD?
A SERIES OF HOME TRUTHS

J. C. Ryle

GLH Publishing
LOUISVILLE, KY

Sourced from the 1852, Robert Carter and Brothers Edition.

GLH Publishing Reprint, 2021

ISBN:
  Paperback 978-1-64863-046-0
  Epub 978-1-64863-047-7

For information on new releases, weekly deals, and free ebooks visit
www.GLHpublishing.com

CONTENTS

I. Living or Dead?......................................1

II. Consider your Ways...........................29

III. Are you Forgiven?............................57

IV. Are you Holy?....................................95

V. Only One Way...................................119

VI. Christ and the Two Thieves.........141

VII. Faith's Choice.................................161

VIII. Remember Lot 180

I. Living or Dead?

"You hath he quickened who were dead."
EPHESIANS II. 1.

READER,—

Look at the words before your eyes, and ponder them well. Search your own heart, and do not lay down this paper without solemn self-inquiry. I meet you this day with one simple question,—Are you among the living, or among the dead?

Listen to me while I try to help you to an answer. Give me your attention, while I unfold this matter, and show you what God has said about it in the Scriptures. If I say hard things, it is not because I do not love you. I write as I do, because I desire your salvation. He is your best friend, who tells you the most truth.

I. First then, *let me tell you what we all are by nature,—we are* DEAD!

"Dead" is a strong word, but it is not my own coining and invention. I did not choose it. The Holy Ghost told Paul to write it down about the Ephesians,—"You hath he quickened who were *dead*." (Eph. ii. 1.) The Lord Jesus Christ made use of it in the parable of the prodigal son,—"This my son was *dead*, and is alive again." (Luke xv. 24, 32.) You will read it also in the Epistle to the Corinthians,—"One died for all, then were all *dead*." (2 Cor. v. 14.) Shall a mortal man be wise above that which is written? Must I not take heed to speak that which I find in the Bible, and neither less nor more?

"Dead" is an awful idea, and one that man is most unwilling to receive. He does not like to allow the whole extent of his soul's disease. He shuts his eyes to the real amount of his danger. Many a one will allow me to say that naturally most people "are not quite what they ought to be,—they are thoughtless,—they are unsteady,—they are gay,—they are wild,—they are not serious enough." But dead? Oh! no! I must not mention it. It is going too far to say that. The idea is a stone of stumbling, and a rock of offence.[1]

My dear Reader, what we like in religion is of very little consequence. The only question is—What is written? What saith the Lord? God's thoughts are not man's thoughts, and God's words are not man's words. God says of every living person, who is not a decided Christian,—be he high or low, rich or poor, old or young,—*he is dead*.

In this, as in everything else, God's words are right. Nothing could be said more correct, nothing more accurate, nothing more faithful, nothing more true. Stay a little, and let me reason this out with you. Come and see.

What should you have said, if you had seen Joseph weeping over his father Jacob?—"He fell upon his face, and wept upon him, and kissed him." (Gen. l. 1.) But there was no reply to his affection. All about that aged countenance was unmoved, silent, and still. Doubtless you would have guessed the reason.—Jacob was dead.

What would you have said, if you had heard the Levite speaking to his wife, when he found her lying before the door in Gibeah? "Up," he said, "and let us be going. But none answered." (Judg. xix. 28.) His words

---

[1] "That is the reason we are no better, because our disease is not perfectly known: that is the reason we are no better, because we know not how bad we are."—*Archbishop Usher's Sermons, preached at Oxford.* 1650.

I. LIVING OR DEAD?

were thrown away. There she lay, motionless, stiff, and cold. You know the cause.—She was dead.

What would you have thought, if you had seen the Amalekite stripping Saul of his royal ornaments in Mount Gilboa? He "took from him the crown that was upon his head, and the bracelet that was on his arm." (2 Sam. i. 10.) There was no resistance. Not a muscle moved in that proud face. Not a finger was raised to prevent him. And why?—Saul was dead.

What should you have thought, if you had met the widow's son in the gate of Nain, lying on a bier, wrapped about with grave-clothes, followed by his weeping mother, carried slowly towards the tomb? (Luke vii. 12.) Doubtless it would have been all clear to you. It would have needed no explanation.—The young man was dead.

Now, I say this is just the condition of every man by nature in the matter of his soul. I say this is just the state of the vast majority of people around us in spiritual things. God calls to them continually,—by mercies, by afflictions, by ministers, by His word;—but they do not hear His voice. The Lord Jesus Christ mourns over them, pleads with them, sends them gracious invitations, knocks at the door of their hearts;—but they do not regard it. The crown and glory of their being, that precious jewel, their immortal soul, is being seized, plundered, and taken away;—and they are utterly unconcerned. The devil is carrying them away, day after day, along the broad road that leads to destruction;—and they allow him to make them his captives without a struggle. And this is going on everywhere,—all around you,—among all classes,—through the length and breadth of the land. You know it in your own conscience, while you read this paper. You must be aware of it. You cannot deny it. And what then, I ask you, can be said more perfectly true than that which God says, We are all by nature spiritually *dead*?

Yes! when a man's heart is cold and unconcerned about religion,—when his hands are never employed in doing God's work,—when his feet are not familiar with God's ways,—when his tongue is seldom or never used in prayer and praise,—when his ears are deaf to the voice of Christ in the Gospel,—when his eyes are blind to the beauty of the kingdom of heaven,—when his mind is full of the world, and has no room for spiritual things,—when these marks are to be found in a man, the word of the Bible is the right word to use about him, and that word is "dead."

We may not like this perhaps. We may shut our eyes both to facts in the world, and texts in the Word. But God's truth must be spoken, and to keep it back does positive harm. Truth must be spoken, however condemning it may be. So long as man does not serve God with body, soul, and spirit, he is not really alive. So long as he puts the first things last and the last first, buries his talent like an unprofitable servant, and brings the Lord no revenue of honor, so long in God's sight he is dead. He is not filling the place in creation for which he was intended. He is not using his powers and faculties as God meant them to be used. The poet's words are strictly true,

> *"He only lives who lives to God,*
> *And all are dead beside."*

This is the true explanation of sin not felt,—and sermons not believed,—and good advice not followed,—and the Gospel not embraced,—and the world not forsaken,—and the cross not taken up,—and self-will not mortified,—and evil habits not laid aside,—and the Bible seldom read—and the knee never bent in prayer. Why is all this on every side? The answer is simple. *Men are dead*.

This is the true account of that host of excuses for neglect of religion, which so many make with one consent. Some have no learning, and some have no time. Some are oppressed with business, and some with poverty. Some have difficulties in their own families, and some in their own health. Some have peculiar obstacles in their calling, which others, we are told, cannot understand; and others have peculiar drawbacks at home, and they wait to have them removed. But God has a shorter word in the Bible, which describes all these people at once. He says, *they are dead*.

This is the true explanation of many things which wring a faithful minister's heart. Many around him never attend a place of worship at all. Many attend so irregularly, that it is clear they think it of no importance. Many attend once on a Sunday, who might just as easily attend twice. Many never come to the Lord's table,—never appear at a week-day means of grace of any kind. And why is all this? Often, far too often, there can only be one reply about these people. *They are dead*.

See now, dear Reader, how all professing Christians should examine themselves and try their own state. It is not in church-yards alone where the dead are to be found. There are only too many inside our churches, and close to our pulpits,—too many on the benches, and too many in the pews. The land is like the valley in Ezekiel's vision, full of bones, and those very dry. There are dead souls in all our parishes, and dead souls in all our streets. There is hardly a family in which all live to God. There is hardly a house in which there is not some one dead. Oh! search and look at home. Prove your own self.

See too how sad is the condition of all who have gone through no spiritual change, whose hearts are still the same as in the day they were born. There is a mountain of division between them and heaven. They have yet to pass from death to life. Oh! that they did but see and know their danger! Alas! it is one fearful mark of spiritual death, that, like natural death, it is not felt. We lay our beloved ones tenderly and gently in their narrow beds, but they feel nothing of what we do. "The dead," says the wise man, "know not anything." (Eccl. ix. 5.) And this is just the case with dead souls.

See too what reason ministers have to be anxious about their congregations. We feel that time is short, and life is uncertain. We know that death spiritual is the high-road that leads to death eternal. We fear lest any of those we preach to should die in their sins, unprepared, unrenewed, impenitent, unchanged. Oh! marvel not if we often speak strongly, and plead with you warmly. We dare not give you flattering titles, amuse you with trifles, say smooth things, and cry peace, peace, when life and death are at stake, and nothing less. The plague is among you. We feel that we stand between the living and the dead. We must and will use great plainness of speech. "If the trumpet give an uncertain sound, who shall prepare himself for the battle?" (1 Cor. xiv. 8.)

II. Let me tell you, in the second place, *what every man needs who would be saved,—he must be quickened and made alive.*

Life is the mightiest of all possessions. From death to life is the mightiest of all changes. And no change short of this will ever avail to fit man's soul for heaven.

Yes! it is not a little mending and alteration,—a little cleansing and purifying,—a little painting and patching,—a little turning over a new leaf, and putting on a new outside, that is wanted. It is the bringing in of something altogether new,—the planting within us a new nature,—a new being,—a new principle,—a new heart,—this alone, and nothing less than this, will ever meet the necessities of man's soul.[2]

---

2 "It is not a little reforming will save the man, no, nor all the morality of the world, nor all the common graces of God's Spirit, nor the outward change of the life: they will not do, unless we are quickened and have a new life wrought in us."—*Usher's Sermons.*

I. Living or Dead?

To hew a block of marble from the quarry, and carve it into a noble statue,—to break up a waste wilderness, and turn it into a garden of flowers,—to melt a lump of iron-stone, and forge it into watch-springs;—all these are mighty changes. Yet they all come short of the change which every child of Adam requires, for they are merely the same thing in a new form, the same substance in a new shape. But man requires the grafting in of that which he had not before. He needs a change as great as a resurrection from the dead. He must become a new creature. Old things must pass away, and all things must become new. He must be born again, born from above, born of God. The natural birth is not a whit more necessary to the life of the body, than is the spiritual birth to the life of the soul.

I know well this is a hard saying. I know well the children of this world dislike to hear they must be born again. It pricks their consciences. It makes them feel they are further off from heaven than they are willing to allow. It seems like a narrow door which they have not yet stooped to enter, and they would fain make the door wider, or climb in some other way. But I dare not give place by subjection in this matter. I will not foster a delusion, and tell people they only need repent a little, and stir up a gift they have within them, in order to become real Christians. I dare not use any other language than that of the Bible. And I say in the words which are written for our learning,—we all need to be born again, we are all naturally dead, and must be made alive.

Reader, if you had seen Manasseh, king of Judah, at one time filling Jerusalem with idols, and murdering his children in honor of false gods, at another purifying the temple, putting down idolatry, and living a godly life;—if you had seen Zacchæus, the publican of Jericho, at one time cheating, plundering, and covetous, at another following Christ, and giving half his goods to the poor;—if you had seen the servants of Nero's household, at one time conforming to their master's profligate ways, at another of one heart and mind with the apostle Paul;—if you had seen the ancient father, Augustine, at one time living in open neglect of the seventh commandment, at another walking closely with God;—if you had seen our own Reformer, Latimer, at one time preaching earnestly against the truth as it is in Jesus, at another spending and being spent even to death in its cause;—if you had seen the New Zealanders, or Tinnevelly Hindoos, at one time blood-thirsty, immoral, and sunk in abominable superstitions, at another holy, pure, and believing Christians;—if you had seen these wonderful changes, or any of them, I ask you what you would have said? Would you have been content to call them nothing more than amendments and alterations? Would you have been satisfied with saying that Augustine had reformed his ways, and Latimer turned over a new leaf? Verily, if you had said no more than this, the very stones would have cried out. I tell you in all these cases there was nothing less than a new birth, a resurrection of human nature, a quickening of the dead. These are the right words to use. All other language is weak, poor, beggarly, unscriptural, and short of the truth.

Now I will not shrink from saying plainly, we all need the same kind of change, if we are to be saved. The difference between us and any of those I have just named, is far less than it appears. Take off the outward crust, and you will find the same nature beneath in us and them, an evil nature requiring a complete change. The face of the earth is very different in different climates, but the heart of the earth, I am told, is everywhere the same. Go where you will, from one end to the other, you would always find the granite rock beneath your feet, if you only bored down deep enough. And it is just the same with men's hearts. Their customs and their colors, their ways and their laws, may all be utterly unlike, but the inner man is always the same;—their hearts are all alike at the bottom, all stony, all hard, all ungodly, all needing to be thoroughly renewed. The Englishman and the New Zealander, stand on the same level in this matter. Both are naturally dead, and both need to be made alive. Both are children of the same father Adam, who fell by sin, and both need to be born again, and made children of God.

Reader, whatever part of the globe we live in, our *eyes* need to be opened: naturally we never see our sinfulness, guilt, and danger. Whatever nation we belong to, our *understandings* need to be enlightened:[3] naturally we know little or nothing of the plan of salvation;—like the Babel-builders, we think to get to heaven our own way. Whatever church we may belong to, our *wills* need to be bent in the right direction;—naturally we should never choose the things which are for our peace,—we should never come to Christ. Whatever be our rank in life, our *affections* need to be turned to things above;—naturally we only set them on things below, earthly, sensual, short-lived, and vain. Pride must give place to humility,—self-righteousness to self-abasement,—carelessness to seriousness—worldliness to holiness,—unbelief to faith. Satan's dominion must be put down within us, and the kingdom of God set up. Self must be crucified, and Christ must reign. Till these things come to pass, we are dead as stones. When these things begin to take place, and not till then, we are alive.

Reader, I dare to say this sounds like foolishness to some. I tell you that many a living man could stand up this day and testify that it is true. Many a one could tell you that he knows it all by experience, and that he does

---

3 "Man's understanding is so darkened that he can see nothing of God in God, nothing of holiness in holiness, nothing of good in good, nothing of evil in evil, nor anything of sinfulness in sin. Nay, it is so darkened that he fancies himself to see good in evil, and evil in good, happiness in sin, and misery in holiness."—*Bishop Beveridge on the Articles.*

indeed feel himself a new man. He loves the things that once he hated, and hates the things that once he loved. He has new habits, new companions, new ways, new tastes, new feelings, new opinions, new sorrows, new joys, new anxieties, new pleasures, new hopes, and new fears.[4] In short, the whole bias and current of his being is changed. Ask his nearest relations and friends, and they would bear witness to it. Whether they liked it or not, they would be obliged to confess he was no longer the same.

Many a one could tell you that once he did not think himself such a very great transgressor. At any rate he fancied he was no worse than others. *Now* he would say, with the apostle Paul, he feels himself the chief of sinners.[5]

Once he did not consider he had a bad heart. He might have his faults, and be led away by bad company

---

4 "How wonderfully doth the new-born soul differ from his former self. He liveth a new life, he walketh in a new way, he steereth his course by a new compass and towards a new coast. His principle is new, his pattern is new, his practices are new, his projects are new, all is new. He ravels out all he had wove before, and employeth himself wholly about another work."—*George Swinnocke*. 1660.

5 "I cannot pray, but I sin: I cannot hear or preach a sermon, but I sin: I cannot give an alms, or receive the sacrament, but I sin: nay, I cannot so much as confess my sins, but my confessions are still aggravations of them. My repentance needs to be repented of, my tears want washing, and the very washing of my tears needs still to be washed over again with the blood of my Redeemer."—*Bishop Beveridge*.

"Woe is me, that man should think there is anything in me! He is my witness, before whom I am as crystal, that the secret house-devils, that bear me too often company, that the corruption which I find within, make me go with low sails."—*Rutherford's Letters*. 1637.

"I am sick of all I do, and stand astonished that the Redeemer still continues to make use of and bless me. Surely I am more foolish than any man; no one receives so much and does so little."—*Whitefield's Letters*.

and temptations, but he had a good heart at the bottom. *Now* he would tell you he knows no heart so bad as his own. He finds it deceitful above all things, and desperately wicked.

Once he did not suppose it was a very hard matter to get to heaven. He thought he had only to repent, and say a few prayers, and do what he could, and Christ would make up what was wanting. *Now* he believes the way is narrow, and few find it. He is convinced he could never have made his own peace with God. He is persuaded that nothing but the blood of Christ could wash away his sins. His only hope is to be justified by faith without the deeds of the law.

Once he could see no beauty and excellence in the Lord Jesus Christ. He could not understand some ministers speaking so much about Him. *Now* he would tell you he is the pearl above all price, the chiefest among ten thousand,—his Redeemer, his Advocate, his Priest, his King, his Physician, his Shepherd, his all.

Once he thought lightly about sin. He could not see the necessity of being so particular about it. He could not think a man's words and thoughts and actions were of such importance, and required such watchfulness. *Now* he would tell you sin is the abominable thing which he hates, the sorrow and burden of his life. He longs to be more holy. He can enter thoroughly into Whitefield's desire, "I want to go where I shall neither sin myself, nor see others sin any more."

Once he found no pleasure in means of grace. The Bible was neglected. His prayers, if he had any, were a mere form. Sermons were a weariness, and often sent him to sleep. *Now* all is altered. These things are the food, the comfort, the delight of his soul.

Once he disliked earnest-minded Christians. He shunned them as melancholy, low-spirited, weak people. *Now* they are the excellent of the earth, of whom he cannot see too much. He is never so happy as he is in their company. He feels if all men and women were saints it would be heaven upon earth.

Once he cared only for this world, its pleasures, its business, its occupations, its rewards. *Now* he looks upon it as an empty, unsatisfying place,—an inn,—a lodging,—a training-school for the life to come. His treasure is in heaven. His home is beyond the grave.

Reader, I ask you once more, what is all this but a new life? Such a change as I have described is no vision and fancy. It is a real actual thing, which not a few in this world have known or felt. It is not a picture of my own imagining. It is a true thing, which many a one could find at this moment hard by his own doors. But wherever such a change does take place, there you see the thing of which I am now speaking,—you see the man made alive, a new man, a new creature, a soul born again.

I would to God that changes such as these were more common! I would to God there were not such multitudes, of whom we must say even weeping, they know nothing about the matter at all. But common or not, one thing I say plainly, this is the kind of change we all need. I do not hold that all must have exactly the same experience. I allow most fully that the change is different, in degree, extent, and intensity, in different persons. Grace may be weak, and yet true;—life may be feeble, and yet real. But I do confidently affirm, we must all go through something of this kind, if ever we mean to be saved. Till this sort of change has taken place, there is no life in us at all. We may be living Churchmen, but we are dead Christians.[6]

Take it home, every man or woman that reads this paper, take it home to your own conscience, and look

---

6 "If we be still our old selves, no changelings at all, the same men that we came into the world, without defalcation of our corruptions, without addition of grace and sanctification, surely we must seek us another Father, we are not yet the sons of God."—*Bishop Hall*. 1652.

at it well. Some time or other, between the cradle and the grave, all who would be saved must be made alive. The words which good old Berridge had graven on his tomb-stone are faithful and true, "Reader, art thou born again? Remember! no salvation without a new birth."

See now, my dear Reader, what an amazing gulf there is between the Christian in name and form, and the Christian in deed and truth. It is not the difference of one being a little better, and the other a little worse than his neighbor.;—it is the difference between a state of life and a state of death. The meanest blade of grass that grows upon a Highland mountain is a more noble object than the fairest wax-flower that was ever formed; for it has that which no science of man can impart,—it has *life*. The most splendid marble statue in Greece or Italy is nothing by the side of the poor sickly child that crawls over the cottage floor; for with all its beauty it is *dead*. And the weakest member of the family of Christ is far higher and more precious in God's eyes, than the most gifted man of the world. The one lives unto God, and shall live forever;—the other, with all his intellect, is still dead in sins.

Oh! you that have passed from death to life, you have reason indeed to be thankful. Remember what you once were by nature,—dead. Think what you are now by grace,—alive. Look at the dry bones thrown up from the graves. Such were ye;—and who has made you to differ? Go and fall low before the footstool of your God. Bless Him for His grace, His free distinguishing grace. Say to Him often, "Who am I, Lord, that thou hast brought me hitherto? Why me, why hast thou been merciful unto me?"

"If thou hast anything less than regeneration, believe me, thou canst never see heaven. There is no hope of heaven till then,—till thou art born again."—*Archbishop Usher's Sermons*.

III. Let me tell you in the third place, *in what way alone this quickening can be brought about,—by what means a dead soul can be made alive.*

Surely, if I did not tell you this, it would be cruelty to write what I have written. Surely, it would be leading you into a dreary wilderness, and then leaving you without bread and water;—it would be like marching you down to the Red Sea, and then bidding you walk over;—it would be commanding you to make brick, like Pharaoh, and yet refusing to provide you with straw;—it would be like tying your hands and feet, and then desiring you to war a good warfare, and so run as to obtain the prize. I will not do so. I will not leave you, till I have pointed out the wicket-gate towards which you must run. By God's help, I will set before you the full provision there is made for dead souls. Listen to me a little longer, and I will once more show you what is written in the Scripture of truth.

One thing is very clear;—we cannot work this mighty change ourselves. It is not in us. We have no strength or power to do it. We may change our sins, but we cannot change our hearts. We may take up a new way, but not a new nature. We may make considerable reforms and alterations. We may lay aside many outward bad habits, and begin many outward duties. But we cannot create a new principle within us. We cannot bring something out of nothing. The Ethiopian cannot change his skin, nor the leopard his spots; no more can we put life into our own souls.[7] (Jer. xiii. 23.)

---

[7] "There is not one good duty which the natural man can do. If it should be said to him, Think but one good thought, and for it thou shalt go to heaven, he could not think it. Till God raise him from the sink of sin, as he did Lazarus from the grave, he cannot do anything that is well-pleasing to God. He may do the works of a moral man but to do the works of a man quickened and enlightened, it is beyond his power."—*Usher's Sermons.*

"Nature can no more cast out nature, than Satan can cast out Satan."—*Thomas Watson.* 1653.

Another thing is equally clear, no man can do it for us. Ministers may preach to you, and pray with you,—receive you at the font in baptism, admit you at the Lord's table, and give you the bread and wine;—but they cannot bestow spiritual life. They may bring in regularity in the place of disorder, and outward decency in the place of open sin. But they cannot go below the surface. They cannot reach your hearts. Paul may plant and Apollos water, but God alone can give the increase. (1 Cor. iii. 6.)

Who then can make a dead soul alive? No one can do it but God. He only who breathed into Adam's nostrils the breath of life, can ever make a dead sinner a living Christian. He only who formed the world out of nothing in the day of creation, can make man a new creature. He only who said, "Let there be light, and there was light," can cause spiritual light to shine into man's heart. He only who formed man out of the dust and gave life to his body, can ever give life to his soul. His is the special office to do it by His Spirit, and His also is the power.[8]

Reader, the glorious Gospel contains provision for your spiritual, as well as your eternal life. The dead must come to Christ, and He will give them life as well as peace. He is able to do everything which sinners need. He cleanses them by His blood,—He makes them alive by His Spirit. The Lord Jesus is a complete Saviour. That mighty living Head has no dead members. His people are not only justified and pardoned, but quickened together with Him, and made partakers of

---

"Nature cannot raise itself to this, any more than a man can give natural being to himself."—*Archbishop Leighton*.

8 "To create or bring something out of nothing, is beyond the power of the strongest creature. It is above the strength of all men and angels to create the least blade of grass; God challengeth this as His prerogative royal. (Isaiah xl. 26.) Augustine said truly, To convert the little world man, is more than to create the great world."—*George Swinnocke*. 1660.

His resurrection. To Him the Spirit joins the sinner, and raises him by that union from death to life. In Him the sinner lives, after he has believed. The spring of all his vitality is the union between Christ and his soul, which the Spirit begins and keeps up. Christ is the appointed fountain of all spiritual life, and the Holy Ghost the appointed agent who conveys that life to our souls.[9]

Come to the Lord Jesus Christ, if you would have life. He will not cast you out. He has gifts, even for the rebellious. The moment the dead man touched the body of Elisha, he revived and stood upon his feet. (2 Kings xiii. 21.) The moment you touch the Lord Jesus with the hand of faith, you are alive unto God, as well as forgiven all trespasses. Come, and your soul shall live.

I never despair of any one becoming a decided Christian, whatever he may have been in days gone by. I know how great the change is from death to life. I know the mountains of division that seem to stand between some of you and heaven. I know the hardness, the prejudices, the desperate sinfulness of the natural heart. But I remember that God the Father made the glorious world out of nothing. I remember the voice of the Lord Jesus could reach Lazarus when four days dead, and recall him even from the grave. I remember the amazing victories the Spirit of God has won in every nation under heaven. I remember all this, and feel that I never need despair. Yes! the very man who now seems most utterly dead in sins, may yet be raised to a new being, and walk before God in newness of life.

Why should it not be so? The Holy Spirit is a merciful and loving Spirit. He turns away from no man because of his vileness. He passes by no one, because his sins are black and scarlet.

---

9 "Then do we begin to live, when we begin to have union with Christ, the Fountain of Life, by His Spirit communicated to us: from this time we are to reckon our life." —*Flavel.*

"Christ is an universal principle of all life." —*Sibbs.* 1635.

I. Living or Dead?

There was nothing in the Corinthians that He should come down and quicken them. Paul reports of them that they were "fornicators, idolaters, adulterers, effeminate, thieves, covetous, drunkards, revilers, extortioners." "Such," he says, "were some of you." Yet even them the Spirit made alive. "Ye are washed," he writes, "ye are sanctified, ye are justified, in the name of the Lord Jesus and by the Spirit of our God." (1 Cor. vi. 9, 10, 11.)

There was nothing in the Colossians, that He should visit their hearts. Paul tells us that "they walked in fornication, uncleanness, inordinate affection, evil concupiscence, and covetousness, which is idolatry." Yet them also the Spirit quickened. He made them "put off the old man with his deeds, and put on the new man which is renewed in knowledge after the image of him that created him." (Coloss. iii. 5–9, 10.)

There was nothing in Mary Magdalene that the Spirit should make her soul alive. Once she had been possessed with seven devils. Time was, if report be true, she had been a woman proverbial for vileness and iniquity. Yet even her the Spirit made a new creature, separated her from her sins, brought her to Christ, made her last at the cross, and first at the tomb.

Never, never will the Spirit turn away from a soul because of its corruption. He never has done so;—He never will. It is His glory that He has purified the minds of the most impure, and made them temples for His own abode. He may yet take the worst man who reads this paper, and make him a vessel of grace.

Why indeed should it not be so? The Spirit is an Almighty Spirit. He can change the stony heart into a heart of flesh. He can break the strongest bad habits like tow before the fire. He can make the most difficult things seem easy, and the mightiest objections melt away like snow in spring. He can cut the bars of brass, and throw the gates of prejudice wide open. He can fill up every valley, and make every rough place smooth. He has done it often, and He can do it again.[10]

The Spirit can take a Jew,—the bitterest enemy of Christianity,—the fiercest persecutor of true believers,—the strongest stickler for Pharisaical notions,—the most prejudiced opposer of Gospel doctrine,—and turn that man into an earnest preacher of the very faith he once destroyed. He has done it already.—He did it with the Apostle Paul.

The Spirit can take a Roman Catholic Monk, brought up in the midst of Romish superstition,—trained from his infancy to believe false doctrine, and obey the Pope,—steeped to the eyes in error,—and make that man the clearest upholder of justification by faith the world ever saw. He has done it already.—He did it with Martin Luther.

The Spirit can take an English tinker, without learning, patronage, or money,—a man at one time notorious for nothing so much as blasphemy and swearing—and make that man write a religious book, which shall stand unrivalled and unequalled in its way by any since the time of the Apostles. He has done so already.—He did it with John Bunyan, the author of "Pilgrim's Progress."

The Spirit can take a sailor, drenched in worldliness and sin,—a profligate captain of a slave-ship,—and make that man a most successful minister of the Gospel,—a writer of letters, which are a store-house of experimental religion,—and of hymns which are known and sung wherever English is spoken. He has done it already.—He did it with John Newton.

All this the Spirit has done, and much more, of which I cannot speak particularly. And the arm of the Spirit is not shortened. His power is not decayed. Such as the Lord Jesus Christ is, such also is the Spirit, the

---

10 "Such is the power of the Holy Ghost to regenerate men, and as it were to bring them forth anew, so that they shall be nothing like the men they were before."—*Homily for Whitsunday*.

same yesterday, to-day, and forever. He is still doing wonders, and will do to the very end.

Once more then, I say, I never despair of any man's soul being made alive. I should if it depended on man himself. Some seem so hardened, I should have no hope. I should if it depended on the work of ministers. Alas! the very best of us are poor, weak creatures. But I cannot despair, when I remember that God the Spirit is the agent who conveys life to the soul, for I know and am persuaded that with him nothing is impossible.

I should not be surprised to hear, even in this life, that the hardest man I ever met, had become softened, and the proudest had taken his place at the feet of Jesus as a weaned child.

I shall not be surprised to meet many on the right hand in the day of judgment, whom I shall leave, when I die, travelling in the broad way. I shall not start, and say, "What! you here!" I shall only remind them, "Was not this my word, when I was yet among you,—nothing is impossible with Him that quickeneth the dead."

Does any one who reads this paper desire to help the Church of Christ? Then pray for a great outpouring of the Spirit. He alone can give edge to sermons, and point to advice, and power to rebukes, and cast down the high walls of sinful hearts. It is not better preaching and finer writing that is wanted in this day, but more of the presence of the Holy Ghost.

Does any one who reads this paper feel the slightest drawing towards God,—the smallest concern about his immortal soul? Then flee to that open fountain of living waters, the Lord Jesus Christ, and you shall receive the Holy Ghost. (John vii. 39.) Begin at once to pray for the Holy Spirit. Think not you are shut up, and cut off from hope. The Holy Ghost is promised to them that ask Him. His very name is the Spirit of promise and the Spirit of life. Give Him no rest till he comes down and makes you a new heart. Cry mightily unto the Lord,—

say unto Him "Bless me, even me also,—quicken me, and make me alive."

And now let me wind up all I have said, with a few words of special application. I have told you what I believe to be the truth as it is in Jesus. Let me try, by God's blessing, to bring it home to your heart.

1. First, let me put this question to every soul who reads this paper,—"Are you living, or are you dead?"

Suffer me, as an ambassador for Christ, to press the inquiry on every conscience. There are only two ways to walk in, the narrow and the broad;—two companies in the day of judgment, those on the right hand and those on the left; two classes of people in the professing Church of Christ, and to one of them you must belong. Where are you? What are you? Are you among the living, or among the dead?

I speak to you yourselves who read this paper, and to none else,—not to your neighbor, but to you,—not to Africans or New Zealanders, but to you. I do not ask whether you are angels, or whether you have the mind of David or Paul,—but I do ask whether you have a well-founded hope that you are new creatures in Christ Jesus,—I do ask whether you have reason to believe you have put off the old man and put on the new,—whether you are conscious of ever having gone through a real spiritual change of heart,—whether, in one word, you are dead or alive?[11]

---

11 "All hangs upon this hinge. If this be not done, ye are undone—undone eternally. All your profession, civility, privileges, gifts, duties, are cyphers, and signify nothing, unless regeneration be the figure put before them."—*Swinnocke*. 1660.

"Believe me, whatsoever thou art, thou shalt never be saved for being a lord, or a knight, a gentleman or a rich man, a learned man or a well-spoken eloquent man; nor yet for being a Calvinist, or a Lutheran, an Arminian, an Anabaptist, a Presbyterian, an Independent, or a Protestant, formally and merely as such;—much less for being a Papist, or of any such grossly deluded sect: but as a regenerate Christian it is that thou must be saved, or thou canst have no hope."—*Richard Baxter*. 1659.

Think not to put me off by saying, "You were admitted into the church by baptism,—you received grace and the Spirit in that sacrament,—you are alive." It shall not avail you. Paul himself says of the baptized widow who lives in pleasure, "She is *dead* while she liveth." (1 Tim. v. 6.) The Lord Jesus Christ himself tells the chief officer of the church in Sardis, "Thou hast a name that thou livest and art *dead*." (Rev. iii. 1.) The life you talk of is nothing if it cannot be seen. Show it to me, if I am to believe its existence. Grace is light, and light will always be discerned. Grace is salt, and salt will always be tasted. An indwelling of the Spirit that does not show itself by outward fruits,—and a grace that men's eyes cannot discover, are both to be viewed with the utmost suspicion. Believe me, if you have no other proof of spiritual life but your baptism, you are yet a dead soul.

Think not to tell me, "It is a question that cannot be decided, and you call it presumptuous to give an opinion in such a matter." This is a vain refuge, and a false humility. Spiritual life is no such dim and doubtful thing as you seem to fancy. There are marks and evidences by which its presence may be discerned by those who know the Bible. "We know, says John, "that we have passed from death unto life." (1 John iii. 14.) The exact time and season of that passage may often be hidden from a man. The fact and reality of it will seldom be entirely an uncertain thing. It was a true and beautiful saying of a Scotch girl to Whitefield, when asked if her heart was changed, "Something was changed, she knew; it might be the world, it might be her own heart; but there was a great change somewhere, she was quite sure, for everything seemed different to what it once did." Oh! cease to evade the inquiry. Anoint your eyes with eye-salve that you may see. Are you dead or alive?

Think not to reply, "You do not know;—you allow it is a matter of importance;—you hope to know some time before you die;—you mean to give your mind to it when you have a convenient season;—but at present you do not know."

You do not know! Yet heaven or hell is wrapped up in this question. An eternity of happiness or misery hinges upon your answer. You do not leave your worldly affairs so unsettled. You do not manage your earthly business so loosely. You look far forward. You provide against every possible contingency. You insure life and property. Oh! why not deal in the same way with your immortal soul?

You do not know! Yet all around you is uncertainty. You are a poor frail worm,—your body fearfully and wonderfully made,—your health liable to be put out of order in a thousand ways. The next time the daisies bloom, it may be over your grave. All before you is dark. You know not what a day may bring forth, much less a year. Oh! why not bring your soul's business to a point without delay?

Reader, begin the great business of self-examination. Rest not till you know the length and breadth of your own state in God's sight. Backwardness in this matter is an evil sign. It springs from an uneasy conscience. It shows that man thinks ill of his own case. He feels like a dishonest tradesman, that his accounts will not bear inquiry. He dreads the light.

Reader, make sure work. Take nothing for granted. Do not measure your condition by that of others. Bring everything to the measure of God's word. A mistake about your soul is a mistake for eternity. "Surely," says Leighton, "they that are not born again, shall one day wish they had never been born."

Sit down this day and think. Commune with your own heart and be still. Go to your own room and consider. Enter into your own closet, or at any rate contrive to be alone with God. Look the question fairly, fully, honestly in the face. How does it touch you? Are you among the living, or among the dead?[12]

2. In the second place, let me speak in full affection to those who are *dead*.

What shall I say to you? What can I say? What words of mine are likely to have any effect on your hearts?

This I will say, I mourn over your souls. I do most unfeignedly mourn. You may be thoughtless and unconcerned. You may care little for what I am saying. You may scarcely run your eye over this paper, and after reading it, despise it, and return to the world; but you cannot prevent my feeling for you, however little you may feel for yourselves.

Do I mourn when I see a young man sapping the foundation of his bodily health, by indulging his lusts and passions, sowing bitterness for himself in his old age? Much more then will I mourn over your souls.

Do I mourn when I see men squandering away their inheritance, and wasting their property on trifles and follies? Much more then will I mourn over your souls.

Do I mourn when I hear of one drinking slow poisons, because they are pleasant, as the Chinese take opium,—putting the clock of his life on, as if it did not go fast enough,—inch by inch digging his own grave? Much more then will I mourn over your souls.

I mourn to think of golden opportunities thrown away,—of Christ rejected,—of the blood of atonement trampled under foot,—of the Spirit resisted,—the Bible neglected,—heaven despised, and the world put in the place of God.

---

12 "If your state be good, searching into it will give you the comfort of it. If your state be bad, searching into it cannot make it worse; nay, it is the only way to make it better; for conversion begins with conviction."—*Bishop Hopkins*. 1680.

I mourn to think of the present happiness you are missing,—the peace and consolation you are thrusting from you,—the misery you are laying up in store for yourselves, and the bitter waking up which is yet to come.

Yes! I must mourn. I cannot help it. Others may think it enough to mourn over dead bodies. For my part, I think there is far more cause to mourn over dead souls. The children of this world find fault with us for being so grave. Truly, when I look at the world, I marvel we can ever smile at all.

Reader, dear Reader, why will you die? Are the wages of sin so sweet and good that you cannot give them up? Is the world so satisfying that you cannot forsake it? Is the service of Satan so pleasant that you and he are never to be parted? Is heaven so poor a thing that it is not worth seeking? Is your soul of so little consequence that it is not worth a struggle to have it saved? Oh! turn, turn, before it be too late. God is not willing that you should perish. "As I live," He says, "I have no pleasure in the death of him that dieth." Jesus loves you, and grieves to see your folly. He wept over wicked Jerusalem, saying, "I would have gathered thee, but thou wouldst not be gathered." Surely if lost, your blood will be upon your own head. "Awake, and arise from the dead, and Christ shall give you light."

Believe me, believe me, true repentance is that one step that no man ever repented. Thousands have said at their latter end, "they have served God too little:" no child of Adam ever said, as he left this world, that he had cared for his soul too much. The way of life is a narrow path, but the footsteps in it are all in one direction,—not one has ever come back and said it was a delusion. The way of the world is a broad way, but millions on millions have forsaken it, and borne their testimony it was a way of sorrow.

Oh! that this year might be a year of life to your soul! Oh! that the Spirit might come down upon your heart, and make you a new man. I ask it of the Lord, as the prophet did of old, "Come from the four winds, O breath, and breathe upon these slain, that they may live." (Ezek. xxxvii. 9.)

3. Let me, in the third place, speak to those who are *living*.

Are you indeed alive unto God? Can you say with truth, I was dead and am alive again, I was blind, but now I see? Then suffer the word of exhortation, and incline your heart unto wisdom.

Are you alive? Then see that you prove it *by your actions*. Be a consistent witness. Let your words, and works, and ways, and tempers all tell the same story. Let not your life be a poor torpid life, like that of a tortoise or sloth;—let it rather be an energetic stirring life, like that of a deer or bird. Let your grace shine forth from all the windows of your conversation, that those who live near you may see that the Spirit is abiding in your hearts. Let your light not be a dim, flickering, uncertain flame, let it burn steadily like the eternal fire on the altar, and never become low. Let the savor of your religion, like Mary's precious ointment, fill all the houses where you dwell. Be an Epistle of Christ, so clearly written, penned in such large bold characters, that he who runs may read it. Let your Christianity be so unmistakable,—your eye so single,—your heart so whole,—your walk so straightforward, that all who see you may have no doubt whose you are, and whom you serve. Oh! dear reader, if we are quickened by the Spirit, no one ought to be able to doubt it. Our conversation should declare plainly that we seek a country. It ought not to be necessary to tell people, as in the case of a badly painted picture, "This is a Christian." We ought not to be so sluggish and still, that men shall be obliged to come close and look hard, and say, "Is he dead or alive?"

Are you alive? Then see that you prove it *by your growth*. Let the great change within become every year more evident. Let your light be an increasing light,—not like Joshua's sun in the valley of Ajalon, standing still,—nor Hezekiah's sun, going back,—but ever shining more and more to the very end of your days. Let the image of your Lord, wherein you are renewed, grow clearer and sharper every month. Let it not be like the image and superscription on a coin, more indistinct and defaced the longer it is used. Let it rather become more plain, the older it is, and the likeness of your King stand out more fully. I have no confidence in a standing-still religion. I do not think a Christian was meant to be like an animal, to grow to a certain age, and then stop growing. I believe rather he was meant to be like a tree, and to increase more and more in strength and vigor all his days. Remember the words of the Apostle Peter, "Add to your faith virtue, and to virtue knowledge, and to knowledge temperance, and to temperance brotherly kindness, and to brotherly kindness charity." (2 Peter i. 5, 6, 7.) This is the way to be a useful Christian. Men will believe you are in earnest when they see constant improvement, and perhaps be drawn to go with you.[13] This is one way to obtain comfortable assurance. "So an entrance shall be ministered unto you abundantly." (2 Peter i. 11.) Oh! as ever you would be useful and happy in your religion, let your motto be, "Forward, forward," to your very last day.

Reader, I speak to myself as well as to you. I say the spiritual life there is in Christians ought to be more evident. Our lamps want trimming,—they ought not to burn so dim. Our separation from the world should be more distinct,—our walk with God more decided.

---

13 "Men who are prejudiced observe actions a great deal more than words."—*Leighton*.

I. LIVING OR DEAD?

Too many of us are like Lot, lingerers,—or like Reuben, Gad, and Manasseh, borderers,—or like the Jews in Ezra's time, so much mixed up with strangers, that our spiritual pedigree cannot be made out. It ought not so to be. Let us be up and doing. If we live in the Spirit, let us also walk in the Spirit. If we really have life, let us make it known.

The state of the world demands it. The latter days have fallen upon us. The kingdoms of the earth are shaking, falling, crashing, and crumbling away. (Isaiah xxiv. 1, etc.) The glorious kingdom that will never be removed is drawing nigh. The King himself is close at hand. The children of this world are looking round to see what the saints are doing. God, in His wonderful providences, is calling to us,—"Who is on my side?" Who?—Surely we ought to be, like Abraham, very ready with our answer, "Here am I."

"Ah!" you may say, "these are ancient things, these are brave words. We know it all. But we are weak, we have no power to think a good thought, we can do nothing, we must sit still." But hear me a little. What is the cause of your weakness? Is it not because the fountain of life is little used? Is it not because you are resting on old experiences, and not daily gathering new manna,—daily drawing new strength from Christ? He has left you the promise of the Comforter. He giveth more grace,—grace upon grace to all who ask it. He came that you might have life, and have it more abundantly. "Open thy mouth wide," He says this day, "and I will fill it." (Psalm lxxxi. 10.)

Reader, if you want your spiritual life to be more healthy and vigorous, you must just come more boldly to the throne of grace. You must give up this hanging back spirit,—this hesitation about taking the Lord at His own word. Doubtless you are a poor sinner, and nothing at all. The Lord knows it, and has provided a store of strength for you. But you do not draw upon the store He has provided; you have not, because you ask not. The secret of your weakness is your little faith, and little prayer. The fountain is unsealed, but you only sip a few drops. The bread of life is before you, yet you only eat a few crumbs. The treasury of heaven is open, but you only take a few pence. O man of little faith, wherefore do you doubt?

Awake to know your privileges;—awake, and sleep no longer. Tell me not of spiritual hunger, and thirst, and poverty, so long as the throne of grace is before you. Say rather, that you are proud, and will not come to it as a poor sinner. Say rather, you are slothful, and will not take pains to get more.

Cast aside the grave-clothes of pride, that still hang around you. Throw off that Egyptian garment of indolence, which ought not to have been brought through the Red Sea. Away with that unbelief, which ties and paralyzes your tongue. You are not straitened in God, but in yourself. Come boldly to the throne of grace, where the Father is ever waiting to give, and Jesus ever stands by Him to intercede. Come boldly, for you may, all sinful as you are, if you come in the name of the Great High Priest. Come boldly, and ask largely, and you shall have abundant answers,—mercy like a river, and grace and strength like a mighty stream. Come boldly, and you shall have supplies exceeding all you can ask or think. Hitherto you have asked nothing. Ask and receive that your joy may be full.

Reader, I commend you to God, and to the Lord Jesus Christ. While you live, may you live unto the Lord. When you die, may you die the death of the righteous. And when the Lord Jesus comes, may you be found ready, and "not be ashamed before Him at His coming."

II. CONSIDER YOUR WAYS

"God is my record how greatly I long after you all."
PHILIPPIANS I. 8.

BELOVED FRIENDS,—

I wish to write a few words to you about your souls. I want those souls to be saved. And I invite you all to take the advice I give you to-day, and that is, to "consider your ways."

I write to you, because the time is short. The day of grace is slipping away,—the day of judgment is drawing near,—the thread of life is winding up,—a few more short years, and every soul of us will have gone to his own place,—we shall each of us be in heaven or hell!

I cannot reach your hearts, I know well. It is not me,—it needs the finger of God. But I can set before you my earnest wishes for every class among you, and I will do it, the Lord being my helper. Bear with me if I say things that sound sharp and hard. Set it down to my anxiety for your salvation;—I mean it all for your good. I write none other things but what I have gathered from the Bible, and as such I commend them to your consciences. Consider what I say, and the Lord give you understanding in all things.

I. First of all let me say, *there are very many among you whom I long to see awakened*.

You are those who have the name of Christians, but not the character which should go with the name. God is not King of your hearts. You mind earthly things. I want you to "consider your ways."

I grant you may be quick and clever about the affairs of this life: you are, many of you, good men of business, good at your daily work, good masters, good servants, good neighbors, good subjects: all this I fully allow. But it is the eternal part of you that I speak of; it is your never-dying soul. And about that, if a man may judge by the little you do for it, you are careless, thoughtless, reckless, and unconcerned.

I do not say that God and salvation are subjects that never come across your minds;—but this I say, they have not the uppermost place there. Neither do I say that you are all alike in your lives;—some of you doubtless go farther in sin than others;—but this I say, you have all turned every one to his own way, and that way is not God's. Brethren, when I look at the Bible I can come to only one conclusion about you,—you are asleep about your souls.

You do not see the sinfulness of sin, and your own lost condition by nature. You appear to make light of breaking God's commandments, and to care little whether you live according to his law or not. Yet God says that sin is the transgression of the law,—that His commandment is exceeding broad,—that every imagination of your natural heart is evil,—that sin is the thing He cannot bear, He hates it,—that the wages of sin is death, and the soul that sinneth shall die. Surely you are asleep!

You do not see your need of a Saviour. You appear to think that it is an easy matter to get to heaven, and that God will of course be merciful to you at last some way or other, though you do not exactly know how. Yet God says that He is just and holy, and never changes,—that Christ is the only way, and none can come unto the Father but by Him,—that without His blood there can be no forgiveness of sin,—that a man without Christ is a man without hope,—that those who would be saved must believe on Jesus, and come to Him,—and that he who believeth not shall be damned. Surely you are asleep!

You do not see the necessity of holiness. You appear to think it quite enough to go on as others do, and live like your neighbors. And as for praying and Bible-reading, making conscience of words and actions, studying truthfulness and gentleness, humility and charity, and keeping separate from the world, they are things you do not seem to value at all. Yet God says, that without holiness no man shall see the Lord,—that there shall enter into heaven nothing that defileth,—that His people must be a peculiar people, zealous of good works. Surely you are asleep!

And, worst of all, *you do not appear to feel your danger*. You walk on with your eyes shut, and seem not to know that the end of your path is hell. Some dreamers fancy they are rich when they are poor, or full when they are hungry, or well when they are sick, and awake to find it all a mistake. And this is the way that many of you dream about your souls; you flatter yourselves you will have peace, and there will be no peace; you fancy that you are all right, and in truth you will find that you are all wrong. Surely you are asleep!

Dear Brethren, what can I say to arouse you? Your souls are in awful peril: without a mighty change they will be lost. When shall that change once be?

You are dying, and not ready to depart;—you are going to be judged, and not prepared to meet God;—your sins are not forgiven, your persons are not justified, your hearts are not renewed. Heaven itself would be no happiness to you if you got there, for the Lord of heaven is not your friend. What pleases Him does not please you. What He dislikes gives you no pain. His word is not your counsellor. His day is not your delight. His law is not your guide. You care little for hearing of Him. You know nothing of speaking with Him. To be forever in His company would be a thing you could not endure; and the society of saints and angels would be a weariness, and not a joy. At the rate you live at, the Bible might never have been written, and Christ might never have died, the Apostles were foolish, the New Testament Christians madmen, and the salvation of the Gospel a needless thing. Oh! awake, and sleep no more!

Think not to say, You cannot believe your case is so bad, or the danger so great, or God so particular. I answer, The devil has been putting this lying delusion into people's hearts for nearly six thousand years. It has been his grand snare ever since the day he said to Eve, "Ye shall not surely die." Do not be so weak as to be taken in by it. God never failed yet to punish sin, and He never will. He never failed to make his word good, and you will find this to your cost one day, except you repent.

And think not to say, You are a member of Christ's Church, and therefore feel no doubt you are as good a Christian as others. I answer, This will only make your case worse, if you have nothing else to plead. You may be written down and registered among God's people; you may be reckoned in the number of the saints; you may sit for years under the sound of the Gospel; you may use holy forms, and even come to the Lord's table at regular seasons;—and still, with all this, unless sin be hateful, and Christ precious, and your heart a temple of the Holy Ghost, you will prove in the end no better than a lost soul. A holy calling will never save an unholy man.

And think not to say, You have been baptized, and so feel confident you are born of God, and have His grace within you. I answer, You have none of the marks which St. John has told me in his first Epistle, distinguish such a person. I do not see you confessing that Jesus is the Christ,—overcoming the world,—not committing sin,—loving your brother,—doing righteousness—keeping yourself from the wicked one. How then can I believe that you are born of God? If God were your Father you would love Christ: if you were God's son you would be led by His Spirit. I want stronger evidences. Show me some repentance and faith; show me a life hid with Christ in God; show me a spiritual and sanctified conversation:—these are the fruits I want to see, if I am to believe you have the root of the matter in you, and are a living branch of the true vine. But without these your baptism will only add to your condemnation.

Beloved Brethren, I speak strongly, because I feel deeply. Time is too short, life is too uncertain, to allow of standing on ceremony. At the risk of offending, I use great plainness of speech. I cannot bear the thought of hearing any of you condemned in the great day of assize;—of seeing any of your faces in the crowd on God's left hand, among those who are helpless, hopeless, and beyond the reach of mercy. I cannot bear such thoughts,—they grieve me to the heart. Before the day of grace is past, and the day of vengeance begins, I call upon you to open your eyes and repent. Oh! *consider your ways* and be wise. Turn ye, turn ye, why will ye die?

This day, as the ambassador of Christ, I pray you to be reconciled to God. The Lord Jesus who came into the world to save sinners,—Jesus, the appointed Mediator between God and man,—Jesus, who loved us, and gave Himself for us,—Jesus sends you all a message of peace; He says, "Come unto me."

"Come" is a precious word indeed, and ought to draw you. You have sinned against heaven,—heaven has not sinned against you; yet, see how the first step towards peace is on heaven's side,—it is the Lord's message, "Come unto me."

"Come" is a word of *merciful invitation*. Does it not seem to say, "Sinner, I am waiting for you, I am not willing that any should perish, but that all should come to repentance. As I live, I have no pleasure in the death of him that dieth. I would have all men saved, and come to the knowledge of the truth. Judgment is my strange work,—I delight in mercy. I offer the water of life to every one who will take it. I stand at the door of your heart and knock. For long time I have spread out my hands to you. I wait to be gracious. There is yet room in my Father's house. My long-suffering waits for more of the children of men to come to the mercy-seat before the last trumpet is blown,—for more wanderers to return before the door is closed forever. Oh! sinner, come to me."

"Come" is a word of *promise and encouragement*. Does it not seem to say, "Sinner, I have gifts ready for you; I have something of everlasting importance to bestow upon your soul; I have received gifts for men, even for the rebellious; I have a free pardon for the most ungodly; a full fountain for the most unclean; a white garment for the most defiled; a new heart for the most hardened; healing for the broken-hearted; rest for the heavy-laden; joy for those that mourn. Oh! sinner, it is not for nothing that I invite you! All things are ready,—come, come unto me."

Beloved Brethren, hear the voice of the Son of God. See that ye refuse not Him that speaketh. Come away from sin, which can never give you real pleasure, and will be bitter at the last. Come out from a world, which will never satisfy you. Come unto Christ. Come with all your sins, however many and however great,—however far you may have gone from God, and however provoking your conduct may have been. Come as you are,—unfit, unmeet, unprepared as you may think yourself,—you will gain no fitness by delay. Come at once, come to the Lord Jesus Christ.

How indeed shall you escape, if you neglect so great salvation? Where will you appear if you make light of the blood of Christ, and do despite to the Spirit of grace? It is a fearful thing to fall into the hands of the living God, but never so fearful as when men fall from under the Gospel. The saddest road to hell is that which runs under the pulpit, past the Bible, and through the midst of warnings and invitations. Oh! beware, lest like Israel at Kadesh, you mourn over your mistake when it is too late; or like Judas Iscariot, find out your sin when there is no space for repentance.

Arise, beloved Brethren, and call upon the Lord. Be not like Esau: sell not eternal blessings for the things of to-day. Surely the time past may suffice you to have been careless and prayerless, Godless and Christless, worldly and earthly-minded: surely the time to come may be given to your soul.

Pray, I beseech you, that you may be enabled to put off the old ways and the old habits, and that you may become new men. I yield to none in wishes for your happiness, and my best wish is that you may be made new creatures in Christ Jesus. This is a better thing than riches, or health, or honor, or learning. A man may get to heaven without these, but he cannot get there without conversion. Verily if you die without having been born again, you had far better never have been born at all.

II. The second thing I have to say is this,—*there are many among you whom I long to see decided followers of Christ*.

You are those who are wavering and halting between two opinions. You seem not to have made up your minds. You appear to stand in doubt which is the true way of serving God, and which the false. One day a man might think you loved Christ,—another he might suppose you did not care for Him at all. You are like the twilight,—I cannot call you darkness,—and yet you are not light in the Lord. There is so much right about you, that I cannot speak to you among the openly ungodly;

and yet there is so much wrong about you, that without a change you will never be saved. I want you also to "consider your ways."

Wavering Brethren, of all classes in the Church, you are the most difficult to address: and no state is so dangerous as yours.

You see something of the evil of sin, and its awful consequences, but not all. You have thoughts about judgment and hell, and you would like to avoid them;—but you never really try.

You see something of the blessedness of heaven, but not all. Its peace, and rest, and joy, and happiness, are things that come across your mind;—but you never really seek to obtain them.

There have been times when you have appeared convinced; there seemed to be much melting and softening going on in your heart. You have been at Sinai, and been alarmed. You have been at Bochim, and wept. You have been at Calvary, and had pricking of conscience. And yet those times have passed away, and your old things still remain.

You have often looked like men going on pilgrimage:—you seemed ready to come out from the world;—and then you have suddenly stopped, and gone no further.

You have done many things that are good,—but unhappily, like Herod, you leave many undone. You give up many habits that are bad, and yet you keep sufficient to make it plain you have no true grace in your hearts.

Oh! wavering Brethren, what can be done for your soul?—I am distressed for you.

Many of you are so like true Christians, that the difference can hardly be seen. You are no opposers of true religion. You have no objection to the preaching of the Gospel, and often take pains to hear it. You can enjoy the company of believers, and appear to take pleasure in their conversation and experience. You can even talk of the things of God as if you valued them. All this you can do.

And yet there is nothing *real* about your religion,—no real witnessing against sin,—no real separation from the world,—no peculiarity,—no warfare. You can wear Christ's uniform in the time of peace, but, like the tribe of Reuben, you are wanting in the day of battle. Times of trouble prove that you were never really on the Rock. Times of sickness and danger bring out the rottenness of your foundations. Times of temptation and persecution discover the emptiness of your professions. There is no dependence to be placed upon you.—Christians in the company of Christians, you are worldly in the company of the worldly. One week I shall find you reading spiritual books, as if you were all for eternity,—another I shall hear of your mixing in some earthly folly, as if you only thought of time. And so you go on, beating about in sight land, but never seeming to make up your mind to come into harbor; showing plainly that you have an idea of the way of life, but not decided enough to act upon your knowledge.

O! wavering Brethren, what can be done for you? I tell you solemnly, I tremble for your souls. In your present course you will never taste peace,—you will go on without comfort, and go off without hope.

Truly you are a wonder in creation. You stand alone. The devil wonders at you, how you can see so much of the way to heaven, and not walk in it. The angels wonder at you, how you can know so much of the Gospel, and yet stand still. Ministers wonder at you, how you can march up to the borders of the promised land, and yet not strive to enter in. Believers wonder at you, how you can taste so much of the good word of God, and yet not determine to eat and live forever. Take heed, lest at last you prove a wonder to yourselves.

Wavering Brethren, let me ask you a simple question. How long do you mean to continue as you are? When do you intend to cease from being *almost* Christians, and become decided? When do you mean to leave Agrippa, and join Paul? You know in your heart and conscience you are not yet saved,—you have no oil in your lamps,—you have not the marks of Christ's people,—you are not true saints. You dare not deny what I say.

When then do you propose to alter? What is the thing that you are waiting for? Oh! turn not away from my question: sit down and answer it if you can.

Are you waiting *till you are sick and unwell*? Surely you will not tell me that is a convenient season. When your body is racked with pain,—when your mind is distracted with all kinds of anxious thoughts,—when calm reflection is almost impossible,—is this a time for beginning the mighty work of acquaintance with God? Do not talk so.

Are you waiting *till you are old*? Surely you have not considered what you say. You will serve Christ when your members are worn out and decayed, and your hands unfit to work. You will go to Him when your mind is weak, and your memory failing. You will give up the world when you cannot keep it. You will set your affections on things above, when you find nothing to set them on in things below. Is this your plan? Beware, lest you insult God.

Are you waiting *till you have leisure*? And when do you expect to have more time than you have now? Every year you live seems shorter than the last: you find more to think of, or to do, and less power and opportunity to do it. And, after all, you know not whether you may live to see another year. Boast not yourself of to-morrow,—now is the time.

Are you waiting *till your heart is perfectly fit and ready*? That will never be. It will always be corrupt and sinful,—a bubbling fountain, full of evil. You will never make it like a pure white sheet of paper, that you can take to Jesus and say, "Here I am, Lord, ready to have thy law written on my heart." Delay not. Better begin as you are.

Are you waiting *till the devil will let you come to Christ without trouble*? That will never be. Satan never gives up a single soul, without a struggle. If you would be saved you must fight for it. Stand not another day. Arise and go forward at once.

Are you waiting *till there is no cross to be borne*? That will never be. So long as sin is our enemy, and our own bodies weak and clogged by it, so long we must endure hardness, if we would be good soldiers of Jesus Christ. Go in the strength of the Lord God, and you shall overcome. If there is no cross there will be no crown.

Are you waiting *till all around you become decided*? That will never be. Heaven only is the place where all are saints. Earth is the place where sin reigns, and God's people are a little flock. You must be content to journey alone, and swim against the stream. "Narrow is the way that leadeth unto life, and few there be that find it." Tarry not for friends and neighbors,—see that you are among the few.

Are you waiting *till the gate is wide*? That will never be. It will not alter,—it is not elastic,—it will not stretch. It is wide enough for the chief of sinners, if he comes in a humble and self-abased spirit. But if there is anything you are resolved not to give up, you will never, with all your struggling, get in. Lay aside every weight,—enter before the door is shut forever.

And are you waiting *because some few Christians are inconsistent, and some professors fall away*? Their folly is no excuse for you. Their sin will not justify your delay. Hear the word of the Lord Jesus, "What is that to thee, follow thou me."

Oh! wavering Brethren, are not your excuses broken reeds—webs that will not cover you—wood, hay, and stubble, that will not abide the fire? Are not your reasonings and defences unprofitable and vain? Be honest,—confess the truth.

Turn not away from good advice. I fear lest the time should come when you will seek to enter in, and not be able. This day I charge you, throw away indecision,—wait no longer, become decided for Christ.

No man is wise till he is decided. What can be more foolish, than to live on in uncertainty? What can be more childish, than to appear not to know what is truth?—to have two ways set before us, and not to be able to decide which is right? Christ is on one side, and the world on the other,—the Bible is on the right hand, and man's opinion on the left: is it not a wonderful and horrible thing that you can think on these things, and yet for a moment doubt? Whether you believe the Gospel true or false, your present position is manifestly wrong. If it be true, you do not go far enough,—if it be false, you go too far. Oh! be decided,—consider your ways and be wise.

No man is safe till he is decided. All are in peril of ruin who are not real followers of Christ,—who are not converted and made children of God.

Wavering Brethren, you fancy there is a middle path between conversion and unconversion. You are mistaken. There seems to be, the devil tells you there is, but in reality there is no such thing. There are but two kingdoms,—Christ's kingdom, and Satan's; there is no neutral ground between:—two parties, believers and unbelievers; there is no third. Consider to which you belong.

Some people, I know, will say you are in a hopeful state. I dare not say so, while you stand still. It would be flattery, and not charity. I tell you rather, your state is dangerous in the extreme. You have enough religion to satisfy you in a way,—you are not as other men, careless, profligate, and the like,—but still you have not enough religion to do you good. You have not the Spirit of Christ, and are none of His.

It is small comfort to my mind to hear that you are not far from the kingdom of God, if you stop there. It wants another step to make you safe, and without that, all the rest is useless. I doubt not many were close to the door of the ark, when the flood came, but all alike were drowned who were not inside. Many, I dare say, came up to the gates of the cities of refuge, but none escaped the destroyer except those who really entered in. Be decided. This is the only way to be safe.

And no man is quite happy in his religion till he is decided. There is little peace so long as you are halting and irresolute. You please no one altogether. Jesus has no consolations for you: He will have all your heart or none. The world is not satisfied with you: they cannot understand your behavior. True Christians dare not comfort you: they can only look on you with suspicion and mistrust. You are like the Samaritans of old, who served the Lord and their own idols at the same time; they formed a middle class between the Jews and Gentiles, and yet were friends with neither;—they were too much Gentiles for the Jews, and too much Jews for the Gentiles. This is just your case. You are trying that which cannot be done; you are trying to serve two masters, and no wonder you are ill at ease.

Wavering Brethren, for your own peace sake, I invite you to choose the better part. Gird up the loins of your mind. Quit you like men. Be strong. God's conduct in punishing sin has ever been decided. Satan's conduct in tempting sinners has ever been decided. Why then are you not decided too?

Cry mightily unto the Lord, that you may be enabled to leave behind your wavering ways. Resolve that, by His grace, you will be true soldiers, real servants, men of God indeed;—that you will never rest until you know in whom you believe. Cease to halt between two opinions. Let your eyes look right on. Cast loose your hold on the world. Lay hold on Christ, and commit yourselves to Him. No man ever came back from the narrow way, and reported that he was sorry for his choice. Thousands have lingered away life, as you are doing now, and have found too late, that the fruit of indecision is eternal sorrow.

III. The last thing I have to say is this, *there are some true Christians among you whom I long to see more holy and more bright*.

You are those who have found out your own sinfulness and lost estate, and really believe on Jesus for the saving of your souls. The eyes of your understanding have been opened by the Spirit,—He has led you to Christ, and you are new men. You have peace with God. Sin is no longer pleasant to you,—the world has no longer the first place in your heart,—all things are become new. You have ceased from trusting in your own works. You are willing to stand before the bar of God, and rest your soul on the finished work of Him who died for the ungodly. This is all your confidence, that you have washed your robes and made them white in the blood of the Lamb. I thank God heartily for what He hath wrought in your souls, but I ask you also to consider your ways.

Believing Brethren, I write to you *about your sanctification*. There are those who think you are a class in our congregations that require little writing to: you are within the pale of salvation—you may be almost let alone. I cannot see it. I believe you need your minister's care and exhortation as much as any, if not more. I believe that on your growth in grace and holiness, not merely your own comfort, but the salvation of many souls, under God, depends. I believe that the converted members of a church should be preached to, spoken to, warned, counselled, far more than they are. You need many words of direction. You are still in the wilderness. You have not crossed Jordan. You are not yet at home.

I see Paul beseeching the Thessalonians that as they have received of Him, how they ought to walk and please God, so they would abound more and more. I see him warning them not to sleep, as others do, but to watch and be sober. I see Peter telling believers to give diligence to make their calling and election sure; to go on adding one grace to another; to grow in grace, and in the knowledge of Christ. I wish to follow in their steps. I would remind you "that this is the will of God, even your sanctification," and I ask you to make it plain it is your will too. You were not chosen out of the world to go to sleep, but that you might be holy. You were not called of God that you might walk worthy of your calling. Recollect those solemn words, "He that lacketh these things is blind and cannot see afar off, and hath forgotten that he was purged from his old sins." (2 Peter i. 9.)

Why do I say these things? Is it because I think you do not know them? No: but I want to stir you up by putting you in remembrance. Is it because I wish to discourage the poor in spirit, and make the heart of the righteous sad? No indeed: I would not willingly do this. Is it because I think true Christians can ever fall away? God forbid you should suppose I mean such a thing.

But I say what I say because *I am jealous for my Lord's honor*. I wish the elect of God to be indeed a holy nation, and the sons of adoption to live as becomes the children of a King. I want those who are light in the Lord to walk as children of light, shining more and more every day.

And I say it *for the good of the world*. You are almost the only book that worldly people read. Surely your lives should be epistles of Christ, so plain that he who runs may read them. The world cares little for doctrine,—the world knows nothing of experience,—but the world can understand a close walk with God.

And not least I say it *because of the times you live in*. I write it down deliberately, I believe there never were so many lukewarm saints as there are now;—there never was a time in which a low and carnal standard of Christian behavior so much prevailed;—there never were so many babes in grace in the family of God,—so many who seem to sit still, and live on old experience,—so many who appear to have need of nothing, and to be neither hungering nor thirsting after righteousness, as at the present time. I write this with all sorrow. It may be too painful to please some. But I ask you, as in God's sight, is it not true?

There is a generation of Christians in this age who grieve me to the heart. They make my blood run cold. I cannot understand them. For anything that man's eye can see, they make no progress. They never seem to get on. Years roll on, and they are just the same,—the same besetting sins, the same infirmities of disposition, the same weakness in trial, the same chilliness of heart, the same apathy, the same faint resemblance to Christ,— but no new knowledge, no increased interest in the kingdom, no freshness, no new strength, no new fruits, as if they grew. Are they not forgetting that growth is the proof of life,—that even the yew-tree grows, and the snail and the sloth move? Are they not forgetting how awfully far a man may go, and yet not be a true Christian? He may be like a waxwork figure, the very image of a believer, and yet not have within him the breath of God:—he may have a name to live, and be dead after all.

Believing Brethren, these are the reasons why I write so strongly. I want your Christianity to be unmistakable. I want you all to grow really, and to do more than others. Let us all henceforth remember Sardis and Laodicea,—let us resolve to be more holy and more bright. Let us bury our idols. Let us put away all strange gods. Let us cast out the old leaven. Let us lay aside every weight and besetting sin. Let us cleanse ourselves from all filthiness of flesh and spirit, and perfect holiness in the fear of God. Let us renew our covenant with our beloved Lord. Let us aim at the highest and best things. Let us resolve by God's blessing to be more holy, and then I know and am persuaded we shall be more useful and more happy.

I name some things for prayerful consideration.

1. Let us then, for one thing, begin with *a humble confession of past unprofitableness and shortcomings*.

Let us acknowledge with shame and contrition that we have not hitherto lived up to our light. We ought to have been the salt of the earth;—but there has been little savor of Christ about us. We ought to have been the light of the world;—but we have most of us been little glimmering sparks that could scarcely be seen. We ought to have been a peculiar people;—but the difference between us and the world has been faint and small. We ought to have been, like Levites, in Israel, a distinct people, among professing Christians:—but we have too often behaved as if we belonged to some other tribe. We ought to have looked on this world as an inn, and we have settled down in it as if it were our home:—it ought to have been counted our school of training for eternity, and we have been at ease in it as if it were our continuing city, or trifled away time in it, as if we were meant to play and not to learn. We ought to have been careful for nothing, and we have been careful and troubled about many things,—we have allowed the affairs of this life to eat out the heart of our spirituality, and have been cumbered with much serving.

How rarely we have heard the Gospel like men in earnest,—and read the Bible as if we were feeding on it,—and prayed as if we wanted an answer! How poor and feeble has been our witness against sin! How seldom have we looked like men about our Father's business! How little have we known about singleness of eye, and wholeness of heart, and walking in the Spirit! How weak has been our faith, how feeble our hope, how cold our charity! How few of us have lived as if we believed all that is written in the Word, and moved through life like pilgrims travelling to a better land!

Oh! Brethren believers, have we not good reason to be ashamed when we think on these things? Very grievous are they, and we ought to feel it. Let us begin with self-abasement,—let us cry "God be merciful to us sinners,—take away our iniquity, for we have done very foolishly."

2. In the next place, *let us all seek to "abide in Christ" more thoroughly than we have hitherto.*

Christ is the true spring of life in every believer's soul, the head on which every member depends, the corner-stone of all real sanctification. Whenever I see a child of God becoming less holy than he was, I know the secret of it,—he is clinging less firmly to Christ than he did. Our root must be right, if our fruit is to abound.

Brethren, let us strive after close union and communion with Christ. Let us go to Him oftener, speak with Him more frequently, trust Him more wholly, look to Him more constantly, lean upon Him more entirely. This is the way to go through the wilderness without fainting, and to run the race set before us with patience. Let us live the life of faith in the Son of God. He is the vine and we are the branches:—let all our strength be drawn from Him: separate from him we can do nothing. He is the Sun of righteousness;—let us seek our comfort in Him, and not in our own frames and feelings. He is the bread of life;—let us feed on Him day by day, as Israel on the manna, and not on our own experiences. Let Christ become more and more all things to us: His blood our peace,—His intercession our comfort,—His word our warrant,—His grace our strength,—His sympathy our support,—His speedy coming our hope. Let others spend their time on new books if they will, let us rather study to learn Christ.

We know a little of Christ as our Saviour, but Oh! how small a portion have we seen of the fulness that is in Him! Like the Indians, when America was first discovered, we are not aware of the amazing value of the gold and treasure in our hands. Believe me, if we did but realize the blessedness of free and full forgiveness in Him, we should be men of a different stamp. The man who *feels* the blood of atonement sprinkled on his conscience,—the man who enjoys assurance that he is washed, and justified, and accepted in the Beloved, this is the man who will be holy indeed, this is the man who will bear much fruit. He will labor cheerfully,—he will suffer patiently,—he will witness confidently,—he will press on unflinchingly,—he will love warmly. Redemption is ever fresh upon his mind, and his thought is, "What shall I render unto the Lord for all his benefits?"

Brethren, let us cleave to Christ more closely. Let us draw nearer to the cross. Let us sit at the feet of Jesus. Let us drink into the spirit of the apostle when he said, "To me to live is Christ." Let us do this, and we shall grow.

3. And let us *beware of excuses*.

Reasons will never be wanting in our minds why we cannot be bright and eminent Christians *just now*. It is very possible to admire a high standard of spirituality in others, while we are content with very low practice ourselves. We persuade ourselves there is something peculiar in our particular case, which makes it almost impossible to shine. But let all excuses be received, like Babylonian ambassadors, with great suspicion. They are generally the devil's coinage. Let us settle it firmly in our hearts, that there are few of us indeed who cannot glorify God just where we are without any change. All our excuses are as dust in the balance when placed against that promise, "My grace is sufficient for thee." Let us not deceive ourselves. By the grace of God we may be bright saints even now.

Let us not say, *"We have bad health."* Remember the apostle Paul:—he had a thorn in the flesh,—some never-ceasing ailment, probably,—and yet it seemed a spur rather than a hindrance to his soul.

Let us not say, *"We have many trials."* Remember Job:—wave upon wave came rolling over him, and yet his faith did not give way; and the record of his patience is on high.

Let us not say, *"We have families and children to make us anxious and keep us back"* Remember David:—none was ever so tried at home as he was, yet he was a man after God's own heart.

Let us not say, *"We have press of distracting business to attend on."* Remember Daniel:—he had far more affairs on his hands probably than any of us, yet he found time to pray three times a day, and was a proverb for godliness.

Let us not say, *"I stand alone, the times are evil, and none around me serve God."* Remember Noah:—the whole world was against him, yet he did not give way. By faith he held fast.

Let us not say, *"We live in families where God is not thought of."* Remember Obadiah in Ahab's house, and Nero's servants at Rome. What are our difficulties compared with theirs?

Let us not say, *"We are poor and unlearned."* Remember Peter and John. They were as poor and unlearned as any of us, yet they were pillars of the early Church, they were of the number of those who turned the world upside down.

No! believing Brethren, such excuses for not being more holy will never do while grace may be had. Let us say rather, "We are slothful and take no trouble,— we are unbelieving and make no bold attempt,—we are worldly and our eyes are too dim to see the beauty of holiness,—we are proud and we cannot humble ourselves to take pains." Let us say this, and we shall more likely speak the truth. There are always ways in which we may glorify God: there are passive graces as well as active. But the way of the slothful is always a hedge of thorns. The wall of Jerusalem was soon built when the Jews had "a mind to work." We complain of the devil, but there is no devil after all like our own hearts. We have not grace because we do not ask it. The fault is all our own.

4. Let us *be on our guard against false doctrine*.

Unsound faith will never be the mother of really sound practice, and in these latter days departures from the faith abound. See then that your loins be girt about with truth, and be very jealous of receiving anything which cannot be proved by the Bible. Think not for a moment that false doctrine will meet you face to face, saying "I am false doctrine, and I want to come into your heart." Satan does not go to work in that way. He dresses up false doctrine like Jezebel,—he paints her face and tires her head, and tries to make her like truth. Think not that those who preach error will never preach anything that is true. Error would do little harm if that was the case. No! error will come before you mingled with much that is sound and scriptural. The sermon will be all right excepting a few sentences. The book will be all good excepting a few pages. And this is the chief danger of religious error in these times,—it is like the subtle poisons of days gone by,—it works so deceitfully that it throws men off their guard. Brethren, take care. Remember that even Satan himself is transformed into an angel of light.

Keep clear of any system of religion which confounds the world and true believers, and makes no broad distinction between those who are true children of God in a congregation, and those who are not. Be not carried away by an appearance of great self-denial and humility. It is far easier to fast and wear sackcloth, and be of a sad countenance, than to receive thoroughly the doctrine of justification by faith without the deeds of the law.

Call no man father upon earth. Build not your faith on any minister or set of ministers. Let no man become your Pope. Make no Christian living your standard of what is right in faith or practice, however high his name, his rank, or his learning. Let your creed be the Bible, and nothing but the Bible; and your example Christ, and nothing short of Him.

Take heed, lest your minds be corrupted from the simplicity that is in Christ. Be careful what books you read on religious subjects: many books of this day are leavened with doctrines which spoil the Gospel. Examine yourselves often whether you are standing in the old paths. Our lost estate by nature,—our recovery through our Saviour's kindness and love,—our need of regeneration and renewal,—our justification through grace;—these are the grand doctrines, as Paul told Titus; and these are the points on which we must be sound, if we would maintain good works.

5. Let us resolve to *make conscience of little things in our daily religion*.

Let us not neglect little duties,—let us not allow ourselves in little faults. Whatever we may like to think, nothing is really of small importance that affects the soul. All diseases are small at the beginning. Many a death-bed begins with "a little cold." Nothing that can grow is large all at once,—the greatest sin must have a beginning. Nothing that is great comes to perfection in a day,—characters and habits are all the result of little actions. Little strokes made that ark which saved Noah. Little pins held firm that tabernacle which was the glory of Israel. We too are travelling through a wilderness,—

let us be like the family of Merari, and be careful not to leave *the pins* behind. (Numbers iv. 32.)

Believers, do not forget how full the Epistles are of instruction about the particulars of Christian life. The apostles seem to take nothing for granted. They do not think it sufficient to say, "be holy,"—they take care to specify and name the things in which holiness is shown. See how they dwell on the duties of husbands and wives, masters and servants, parents and children, rulers and subjects, old people and young. See how they single out and urge upon us industry in business, kindness in temper, forgiveness in disposition, honesty, truthfulness, temperance, meekness, gentleness, humility, charity, patience, courtesy. See how they exhort us to honor all men, to govern our tongues, to season our speech with grace, to abstain from foolish talking and jesting, not to please ourselves only, to redeem the time, to be content with such things as we have, and whether we eat or drink to do all in the name of the Lord Jesus.

Brethren, some people think that to dwell on such things is bondage; but I believe it good to remind you of them,—I am sure it is safe. If the Spirit of God thought it wise to dwell so much on them in the word, I cannot doubt it must be wise for us to attend to them in our walk. It is much more easy to profess holiness in a general way, than to carry it out in particulars; and I fear that many talk familiarly of santification in the *lump*, who know but little of it in the *piece*.

I firmly believe that looseness about these little things in our daily behavior, is a special means of grieving the Spirit of God, and of bringing upon us in consequence barrenness and leanness of soul.

6. Let us be *more active in endeavors to do good to the world*.

Surely we may all do far more for unconverted souls than we have ever done yet. Many of us, alas! take things so quietly, that a man might suppose every one about us was converted, and the kingdom of Christ fully set up. I pray you let us lay aside these lazy habits.

Are all our friends and relations in Christ? Are all our neighbors and acquaintances inside the ark? Have all within our reach received the truth in the love of it? Have we asked them all to come in? Have we told them all the way of salvation, and our own experience that the way is good? Have we done all that we can? Have we tried every means? Is there no one left to whom we can show Christian kindness, and offer the Gospel? Can we lift up our hands to God, as one by one, souls around us are taken away, and say, "Our eyes, O Lord, have not seen this blood, and its loss cannot in any wise be laid at our door!" Surely, my Brethren, grace ought to be as active a principle in trying to spread godliness, as sin is in trying to spread evil. Surely if we had a tenth part of the zeal which Satan shows to enlarge his kingdom, we should be far more full of care for other men's souls. Where is our mercy and compassion, if we can see disease of soul about us, and not desire to make it less?

Let us awake to a right understanding of our responsibility in this matter. We complain of the world being full of wickedness. It is so. But do we each do our own part in trying to make it better? Do we act upon the old saying, "The city is soon clean when every man sweeps before his own door?" Let us try more to do good to all. Let us reckon it a painful thing to go to heaven alone,—let us endeavor, as far as we can, to take companions with us. Let us no longer be silent witnesses and muffled bells. Let us warn, and beseech, and invite, and rebuke, and advise, and testify of Christ, on the right hand and on the left, according as we have opportunity,—saying to men, "Come with us, and we will do you good,—the light is sweet, come and walk in the light of the Lord." Let us not suppose no good is done in this way, because our eyes do not see it: we must walk by faith, and not by sight. Let us not be weary in well-doing, because we appear to labor in vain; we may rest assured we are in the hands of a good Master,—in due time we shall reap if we faint not.

Activity in doing good is one receipt for being cheerful Christians: it is like exercise to the body,—it keeps the soul in health.

It is one great proof of love toward the Lord Jesus, and a proof that can only be given while we are alive. *Now* is the time for doing good to others, and not hereafter. In heaven there will be no missionary societies, no Bible societies, no visiting societies, no careless to warn, no ignorant to instruct, no sick to minister to, no mourners to comfort, no fainting saints to cheer. In heaven there will be love, joy, peace, thankfulness; but in heaven there will be no place for faith, zeal, courage, labor patience,—their occupation will be over:—if ever we mean to show these graces it must be *now*. Oh! let us make haste, for the time is short. Let us be like Christian, in Pilgrim's Progress,—when his burden fell off at the sepulchre, his first act was to try to awaken sleeping souls.

7. Lastly, let us *take more pains to edify other believers*.

It is wonderful and sad to see how Scripture speaks on this matter, and then to observe the conduct of many of Christ's people.

Paul tells the Corinthians, that the members of Christ "should have the same care one for another." He says to the Thessalonians, "Edify one another, even as also ye do." He says to the Hebrews, "Exhort one another daily, lest any be hardened through the deceitfulness of sin," and again, "Consider one another to provoke unto love and good works;—exhorting one another, and so much the more as ye see the day approaching."

Brethren, I fear we fall very short of the New Testament Christians in this respect. We are sadly apt to lose sight of this edifying one another, when we are in the company of believing friends. Prayer, and the Word, and godly conversation, are not put in the foremost place, and so we separate, nothing better, but rather worse. Far too often there is so much coldness, and restraint, and reserve, and backwardness, that a man might fancy we were ashamed of Christ, and that we thought it proper to hold our tongues, and not make mention of the name of the Lord.

These things ought not so to be. We profess that we are all fighting the same fight,—contending with the same enemies,—plagued with the same evil hearts,—trusting in the same Lord, led by the same Spirit,—eating the same bread,—journeying towards the same home. Then why should we not show it? Why should we not be always ready to commune with each other? Why should we not try to help each other forward,—to profit by each other's experience,—to bear each other's burdens,—to strengthen each other's hands,—to quicken each other's hearts,—to speak with each other, like Moses and Jethro, of the things pertaining to our King. There is a fault among us here, and one that ought to be amended.

Let us bring out the Bible more when we get together. We none of us know it all yet; our brother may have found some pearl in it which has escaped our eyes, and we perhaps may show him something in return. It is the common map by which we all journey; let us not behave as if we had each a private map to be studied in a corner, and kept to ourselves. Oh! that the Word were like a burning fire shut up in our bones, so that we could not forbear speaking of it!

Let us speak oftener about the eternal home towards which we travel. Children, before their holidays, love to talk of home,—their hearts are full, they cannot help it,—why should not we? Surely it ill becomes the citizens of heaven to say nothing of heaven to those with whom they expect to dwell forever.

Let us aim at closer communion with all true believers. This will go far to procure Christ's presence with us on our journey. The two disciples who went to Emmaus were talking of holy things when they were joined by the Lord. Let us speak often one to another, and the Lord will hearken and remember it. This too will mightily promote the growth and comfort of our souls. The fire within us needs constant stirring, as well as feeding, to keep it bright. Many can testify that they find communion a special means of grace. As iron sharpeneth iron, so doth the countenance of a man his friend;—and the weakest too may sharpen the strongest, even as the whetstone does the scythe. He that tries to promote holiness in others shall reap a blessed reward in his own soul,—he waters others, and he shall be watered himself.

Brethren believers, I have thought it good to name these things in writing to you about sanctification. I desire to do it in all humility. I need reminding of them as much as any. Let us all resolve to set them before us, and I am sure we shall not repent it.

And now, beloved Brethren, I have done; I have told you one and all the longings and de sires of my heart. Conversion for the unconverted, decision for the wavering, growth in grace for the believer,—this seals up the sum of my wishes for you.

I *can* wish you nothing better, for this is the way to true happiness. I *will* wish you nothing less, for without these things I am sure there is no peace. Consider well what I have said.

Death *may* be busy among us very soon,—let us all be found in Christ and prepared. Satan *will* be busy among us no doubt,—let us all watch and pray. Let us beware of a spirit of slumber and formality, and especially in private reading and praying. Let our path to the fountain be worn with daily journeys, let our key to the treasury of grace be bright with constant use. Let us pray more, and let us pray more earnestly. Let those who never prayed begin to pray. Let those who have prayed pray better.

Pray for *yourselves*,—that you may know the Lord Jesus, and cleave to Him,—that you may be kept from falling,—that you may serve your generation,—that you may be sober in prosperity, patient in trial, and humble at all times.

Pray for the *congregation* to which you belong,—that the word of the Lord may have free course in it, and be glorified, that the household of faith may become stronger and stronger, and the household of unbelief weaker and weaker.

Pray for *your country*,—that her ministers may preach the Gospel, and be sound in the faith,—that her rulers may value the Bible, and govern according to it,—and that so her candlestick may not be taken away.

And pray not least for *your minister*, that he may be strong to work, and willing to labor for your good,—that all his sicknesses may be sanctified, and all his health given to the Lord,—that he may be ever taught of the Spirit, and thus be able to teach others,—that he may be kept faithful unto death, and so be ready to depart when he is called.

Let us all pray, one for the other,—I for you, and you for me,—and we shall be blessed in our deed.

III. ARE YOU FORGIVEN?

"Your sins are forgiven you."
1 JOHN II. 12.

READER,—

Do you see the question which stands at the head of this page? It is just possible you may not understand its meaning. Perhaps you may think, "Whom have I injured? Whom have I defrauded? Whom have I wronged? Whose confidence have I forfeited? What need have I of forgiveness?"

I answer, it is not an earthly forgiveness I am asking about, but a heavenly one. I do not inquire whether you are forgiven in the sight of men, but whether you are forgiven in the sight of God. The question I desire to press home on your conscience is simply this, *"Are you a pardoned soul?"*

Come, now, and give me your attention, while I speak to you about the forgiveness of sins. The subject is one which can never be considered too soon. We lately saw the pestilence slaying its thousands and tens of thousands of our countrymen. The strongest were carried off in a few hours. The cleverest physicians found their skill entirely unavailing. We live yet, and we may well be thankful. We live yet, and surely we should be thoughtful. Our turn may come next. Our graves may soon be ready for us. Come then, I say once more, and let me speak to you about the forgiveness of sins.

1. *Let me show you first of all your need of forgiveness.*

All men need forgiveness, because all men are sinners. He that does not know this, knows nothing in religion. It is the very A B C of Christianity, that a man should know his right place, and understand his deserts.

We are *all great sinners*. Sinners we were born, and sinners we have been all our lives We take to sin naturally from the very first No child ever needs schooling and education to teach it to do wrong. No devil or bad companion ever leads us into such wickedness as our own hearts. And yet the wages of sin is death. We must either be forgiven, or lost eternally.[14]

We are *all guilty sinners* in the sight of God. We have broken His holy law. We have transgressed His precepts. We have not done His will. There is not a commandment in all the ten that does not condemn us. If we have not broken it in deed, we have in word. If we have not broken it in word, we have in thought and imagination,—and that continually. Tried by the standard of the fifth chapter of St. Matthew, there is not one of us that would be acquitted. And yet it is appointed unto men once to die, and after this comes the judgment. We must either be forgiven, or perish everlastingly.

When I walk through the crowded streets of London, I see hundreds and thousands, of whom I know nothing beyond their outward appearance. I see some bent on pleasure, and some on business,—some who look rich, and some who look poor,—some rolling in their carriages, some hurrying along on foot. Each has his own object in view. Each has his own aims and ends, all alike hidden from me. But one thing I know for a certainty, as I look upon them, they are all sinners. There is not a soul among them all but is guilty

---

14 "No man that seeth himself to be a sinner really, can count himself a small or little sinner. Nor can it ever be, till there be a little law to break, a little God to offend, a little guilt to contract, and a little wrath to incur. All which are impossible to be, blasphemy to wish, and madness to expect." —*Traill*. 1690.

before God. There breathes not the man or woman in that crowd, but must die *forgiven*, or else rise again to be condemned forever at the last day.

When I look through the length and breadth of Great Britain, I must make the same report. From the Land's End to the North Foreland,—from the Isle of Wight to Caithness,—from the Queen on the throne to the pauper in the workhouse,—we are all sinners. We have got a name among the Empires of the earth. We send our ships into every sea, and our merchandise into every town in the world. We have bridged the Atlantic with our steamers. We have made night in our cities like day with gas. We have changed England into one great county by railways. We can exchange thought between London and Edinburgh in a few seconds by the electric telegraph. But with all our arts and sciences,—with all our machinery and inventions,—with all our armies and navies,—with all our lawyers and statesmen, we have not altered the natures of our people;—we are still in the eye of God an island full of sinners.

When I turn to the map of the world, I must say the same thing. It matters not what quarter I examine, I find men's hearts are everywhere the same, and everywhere wicked. Sin is the family disease of all the children of Adam. Never has there been a corner of the earth discovered, where sin and the devil do not reign. Wide as the differences are between the nations of the earth, they have been found to have one great mark in common. Europe and Asia, Africa and America, Iceland and India, Paris and Pekin, all alike have the mark of sin. The eye of the Lord looks down on this globe of ours, as it rolls round the sun, and sees it covered with corruption and wickedness. What he sees in the moon and stars, Jupiter and Saturn, I cannot tell,—but on the earth I know He sees sin. (Psalm xiv. 2, 3.)

Reader, you may not perhaps like what I am saying. I have no doubt such language as this sounds extravagant to some. You think I am going much too far. But mark well what I am about to say next, and then consider whether I have not used the words of soberness and truth.

What then, I ask, is *the life of the best Christian amongst us all*? What is it but one great arrear,—one long catalogue of shortcomings? What is it but a daily acting out the words of our Prayer Book, "leaving undone things that we ought to do, and doing things that we ought not to do?" Our faith, how feeble! Our love, how cold! Our works, how few! Our zeal, how small! Our patience, how short-breathed! Our humility, how threadbare? Our self-denial, how dwarfish! Our knowledge, how dim! Our spirituality, how shallow! Our prayers, how formal! Our desires for more grace, how faint! Never did the wisest of men speak more wisely than when he said, "There is not a just man upon earth that doeth good and sinneth not." (Eccles. vii. 20.) "In many things," says the apostle James, "we offend all." (James iii. 2.)

And *what is the best action* that is ever done by the very best of Christians? What is it after all but an imperfect work, when tried on its own merits? It is, as Luther says, no better than a splendid sin. It is always more or less defective. It is either wrong in its motive, or incomplete in its performance,—not done from perfect principles, or not executed in a perfect way. The eyes of men may see no fault in it, but weighed in the balance of God it would be found wanting, and viewed in the light of heaven, it would prove full of flaws. It is like the drop of water which seems clear to the naked eye, but placed under a microscope is discovered to be full of impurity. David's account is literally true, "There is none that doeth good, no not one." (Psalm xiv. 3.)[15]

---

15 "Let us acknowledge ourselves before God, as we be indeed, miserable and wretched sinners. Let us all confess with mouth and heart, that we be full of imperfections. There be imperfec-

And then, *what is the Lord God*, whose eyes are on all our ways, and before whom we have one day to give account? "Holy, holy, holy," is the remarkable expression applied to Him by those who are nearest to Him. (Isaiah vi. 3.; Rev. iv. 8.) It sounds as if no one word could express the intensity of His holiness. One of His prophets says, "He is of purer eyes than to behold evil, and cannot look on iniquity." (Habak. i. 13.) We think the angels exalted beings, and far above ourselves; but we are told in Scripture, "He charged His angels with folly." (Job iv. 18.) We admire the moon and stars as glorious and splendid bodies, but we read, "Behold, even to the moon, and it shineth not; yea, the stars are not pure in His sight." (Job xxv. 5.) We talk of the heavens as the noblest and purest part of creation; but even of them it is written, "The heavens are not clean in His sight." (Job xv. 14.) Reader, what is any of us but a miserable sinner in the sight of such a God as this?

Surely we ought all to cease from proud thoughts about ourselves. We ought to lay our hands upon our mouths, and say with Abraham, "I am dust and ashes," and with Job, "I am vile," and with Isaiah, "We are all

---

tions in our best works; we do not love God so much as we are bound to do, with all our heart, mind, and power: we do not fear God so much as we ought to do: we do not pray to God, but with many and great imperfections; we give, forgive, believe, live, and hope imperfectly: we speak, think, and do imperfectly: we fight against the devil, the world, and the flesh imperfectly. Let us not be ashamed to confess imperfection, even in all our own best works." — *Church of England Homily on the Misery of Man.*

"If God should make us an offer thus large, Search all the generations of men since the fall of your father Adam, find one man that hath done any one action, which hath past from him pure, without any stain or blemish at all; and for that one man's one only action, neither man nor angel shall feel the torments which are prepared for both: do you think this ransom, to deliver men and angels, would be found among the sons of men? The best things we do have somewhat in them to be pardoned. How then can we do anything meritorious, and worthy to be rewarded?" — *Richard Hooker.* 1585.

as an unclean thing," and with John, "If we say that we have no sin we deceive ourselves, and the truth is not in us." (Gen. xviii. 27; Job xl. 4; Isaiah lxiv. 6; 1 John i. 9.) Where is the man or woman in the whole catalogue of the Book of life, that will ever be able to say more than this. "I obtained mercy?" What is the glorious company of the apostles, the goodly fellowship of the prophets, the noble army of martyrs,—what are they all but pardoned sinners? Surely there is but one conclusion to be arrived at,—we are all great sinners, and we all need a great forgiveness.[16]

See now what just. cause I have to tell you that to know your need of forgiveness, is the first thing in true religion. Sin is a burden, and must be taken off. Sin is a defilement, and must be cleansed away. Sin is a mighty debt, and must be paid. Sin is a mountain standing between us and heaven, and must be removed. Happy is that mother's child amongst us that feels all this! The first step towards heaven is to see clearly that we *deserve hell*. There is but one alternative before us,—we must be forgiven, or be miserable forever.[17]

See too how little many persons know of the design of Christianity, though they live in a Christian land. They fancy they are to go to church to learn their duty, and hear morality enforced, and for no other purpose. They forget that the heathen philosophers could have told them as much as this. They forget that such men as Plato and Seneca gave instruction, which ought to put to shame the Christian liar, the Christian drunkard,

---

[16] "Who is in this world, or ever hath been, which hath not need to say this prayer;—to desire God to take from him his sins, to forgive him his trespasses? Truly no saint in heaven, be they as holy as ever they will, but they have had need of this prayer; they have had need to say, Lord forgive us our trespasses."—*Bishop Latimer's Sermons*. 1552.

[17] "No man shall be in heaven but he that sees himself fully qualified for hell, as a fagot that is bound up for eternal burnings, unless mercy plucks the brand out of the fire."—*Traill*. 1690.

and the Christian thief. They have yet to learn that the leading mark of Christianity is the *remedy* it provides for sin. This is the glory and excellence of the Gospel. It meets man as he really is. It takes him as it finds him. It goes down to the level to which sin has brought him, and offers to raise him up. It tells him of a remedy equal to his disease—a great remedy for a great disease,—a great forgiveness for great sinners.

Reader, I ask you to consider these things well, if you have not considered them before. It is no light matter whether you know your soul's necessities or not. It is a matter of life and death. Try, I beseech you, to become acquainted with your own heart. Sit down and think quietly what you are in the sight of God. Bring together the thoughts and words and actions of any day in your life, and measure them by the measure of God's word. Judge yourself honestly, that you may not be condemned at the last day. O that you may find out what you really are! O that you may learn to pray Job's prayer, "Make me to know my transgression and my sin." (Job xiii. 23.) O that you may see this great truth, that until you are *forgiven*, your Christianity has done nothing for you at all.

II. *Let me point out to you, in the second place, the way of forgiveness.*

I ask your particular attention to this point, for none can be more important. Granting for a moment that you want pardon and forgiveness, what ought you to do? Whither will you go? Which way will you turn? Everything hinges on the answer you give to this question.

Will you turn to *ministers*, and put your trust in them? They cannot give you pardon: they can only tell you where it is to be found. They can set before you the bread of life: but you yourself must eat it. They can show you the path of peace: but you yourself must walk into it. The Jewish priest had no power to cleanse the leper, but only to declare him cleansed. The Christian minister has no power to forgive sins,—he can only pronounce who they are that are forgiven.[18]

Will you turn to *sacraments and ordinances*, and trust in them? They cannot supply you with forgiveness, however diligently you may use them. By sacraments faith is confirmed and grace increased, in all who rightly use them. But they cannot justify the sinner. They cannot put away transgression. You may go to the Lord's table every Sunday in your life; but unless you look far beyond the sign to the thing signified, you will after all die in your sins.[19] You may attend a daily service regularly, but if you think to establish a righteousness of your own by it in the slightest degree, you are only getting further away from God every day.

Will you trust in your own *works and endeavors*, your virtues and your good deeds, your prayers and your alms? They will never buy for you an entrance into heaven. They will never pay your debt to God. They are all imperfect in themselves, and only increase your guilt. There is no merit or worthiness in them at the very best. "When ye have done all those things

---

18 "Ministers cannot remit sin, authoritatively and effectually, but only declaratively. They have a special office and authority to apply the promises of pardon to broken hearts. When a minister sees one humbled for sin, yet afraid God hath not pardoned him, and ready to be swallowed up of sorrow, in this case a minister for the easing of the man's conscience may, in the name of Christ, declare to him that he is pardoned. The minister doth not forgive sin by his own authority, but as a herald in Christ's name pronounceth the man's pardon."—*Thomas Watson*. 1660.

19 "He that supposeth to make Christ his, and all Christ's merits, by the receiving of the outward sign and sacrament, and bringeth not Christ in his heart to the sacrament, he may make himself assured rather of the devil and eternal death, as Judas and Cain did. For the sacrament maketh not the union, peace, and concord between God and us, but it ratifieth, establisheth, and confirmeth the love and peace that is between God and us *before* for His promise sake."—*Bishop Hooper*. 1545.

which are commanded you," says the Lord Jesus, "say we are unprofitable servants."[20] (Luke xvii. 10.)

Will you trust in your own *repentance and amendment*? You are very sorry for the past. You hope to do better for time to come. You hope God will be merciful. Alas! if you lean on this, you have nothing beneath you but a broken reed. The judge does not pardon the thief because he is sorry for what he did. To-day's sorrow will not wipe off the score of yesterday's sins. It is not an ocean of tears that will ever cleanse an uneasy conscience, and give it peace.

Where then must a man go for pardon? Where is forgiveness to be found? Listen, Reader, and by God's help I will tell you. There is a way both sure and plain, and into that way I desire to guide every inquirer's feet.

That way is, simply to trust in the Lord Jesus Christ, the Son of God, as your Saviour. It is to cast your soul, with all its sins, unreservedly on Christ,—to cease completely from any dependence on your own works and doings, either in whole or in part, and to rest on no other work but Christ's work, no other righteousness but Christ's righteousness, no other merit but Christ's merit, as your ground of hope. Take this course, and you are a pardoned soul. "To Christ," says Peter, "give all the prophets witness, that through His name whosoever believeth in Him shall receive remission of sins." (Acts x. 43.) "Through this man," said Paul at Antioch,

---

20 "What if I should fast my body into a skeleton, and pray my tongue and wear my ears to their very stumps? What though I should water my couch continually with my tears, fasten my knees always to the earth by prayer, and fix my eyes constantly into heaven by meditation? What though I should give everything I have to my poor distressed neighbors, and spend each moment of my time in the immediate worshipping of my glorious Maker? Would any of this be more than I am bound to do? Should I not still be an unprofitable servant? And if I can do more than is my duty unto God, how can I merit anything by what I do for Him? How can He be indebted to me for my paying what I owe to Him?"—*Bishop Beveridge*. 1700.

"is preached unto you the forgiveness of sins, and by Him all that believe are justified from all things." (Acts xiii. 38.) "In Him," writes Paul to the Colossians, "we have redemption through His blood even the forgiveness of sins." (Col. i. 4.)

The Lord Jesus Christ, in great love and compassion, has made a full and complete satisfaction for sin, by His own death upon the cross. There He offered Himself as a sacrifice for us, and allowed the wrath of God which we deserved, to fall on His own head. For our sins He gave Himself, suffered, and died,—the just for the unjust, the innocent for the guilty,—that He might deliver us from the curse of a broken law, and provide a complete pardon for all who are willing to receive it. And by so doing, as Isaiah says, He has *borne* our sins,—as John the Baptist says, He has *taken away* sin,—as Paul says, He has *purged* our sins, and *put away* sin,—and as Daniel says, He has *made an end of sin*, and *finished* transgression. (Isaiah liii. 11. John i. 29. Heb. i. 3; ix. 26. Dan. ix. 24.)

And now the Lord Jesus is sealed and appointed by God the Father to be a Prince and a Saviour, to give remission of sins to all who will have it. The keys of death and hell are put in His hand. The government of the gate of heaven is laid on His shoulder. He Himself is the door, and by Him all that enter in shall be saved. (Acts v. 31. Rev. i. 18. John x. 9.)

Christ, in one word, has purchased a full forgiveness, if you and I are willing to receive it. He has done all, paid all, suffered all that was needful to reconcile us to God. He has provided a garment of righteousness to clothe us. He has opened a fountain of living waters to cleanse us. He has removed every barrier between us and God the Father, taken every obstacle out of the way, and made a road by which the vilest may return. All things are now ready, and the sinner has only to believe and be saved, to eat and be satisfied, to ask and receive, to wash and be clean.

And faith, simple faith, is the only thing required, in order that you and I may be forgiven. That we will come to Jesus as sinners with our sins,—trust in Him,—rest on Him,—lean on Him,—confide in Him,—commit our souls to Him,—and *forsaking all other hope, cleave only to Him*,—this is all and everything that God asks for. Let a man only do this, and he shall be saved. His iniquities shall be found completely pardoned, and his transgressions entirely taken away. Every man that so trusts is wholly forgiven, and reckoned perfectly righteous. His sins are clean gone, and his soul is justified in God's sight, however bad and guilty he may have been.[21]

---

21 "We must only trust to the merits of Christ, which satisfied the extreme jot and uttermost point of the law for us. And this His justice and perfection He imputeth and communicateth with us by faith. Such as say that only faith justifieth not, because other virtues be present, they cannot tell what they say. Every man that will have his conscience appeased must mark these two things: How remission of sins is obtained, and wherefore it is obtained. Faith is the *mean* whereby it is obtained, and the *cause* wherefore it is received is the merits of Christ."—*Bishop Hooper.* 1547.

"When we believe in Christ, it is like as if we had no sins. For He changeth with us: He taketh our sins and wickedness from us, and giveth unto us His holiness, righteousness, justice, fulfilling of the law, and so consequently everlasting life. So that we be like as if we had done no sin at all; for His righteousness standeth us in good stead, as though we of our own selves had fulfilled the law to the uttermost."—*Bishop Latimer. Sermons.* 1549.

"The spiritual hand whereby we receive the sweet offer of our Saviour is faith; which in short is no other than an affiance in the Mediator. Receive peace, and be happy; believe, and thou hast received."—*Bishop Hall.* 1640.

"Justifying faith consists in these two things, in having a mind to know Christ, and a will to rest upon Him. Whosoever sees so much excellency in Christ, that thereby he is drawn to embrace Him as the only Rock of salvation, that man truly believes to justification."—*Archbishop Usher.* 1670.

Faith is the only thing required, *not knowledge*. A man may be a poor unlearned sinner, and know little of books. But if he sees enough to find the foot of the cross, and trust in Jesus for pardon, I will engage he shall not miss heaven. To know Christ is the cornerstone of all religious knowledge.

Faith, I say, and *not conversion*. A man may have been walking in the broad way up to the very hour he first hears the Gospel. But if in that hearing he is awakened to feel his danger, and wants to be saved, let him come to Christ at once, and wait for nothing. That very coming is the beginning of conversion.

Faith, I repeat, and *not holiness*. A man may feel all full of sin, and unworthy to be saved. But let him not tarry outside the ark till he is better. Let him come to Christ without delay, just as he is. Afterwards he shall be holy.

Reader, I call upon you to let nothing move you from this strong ground, that *faith in Christ is the only thing needed for your justification*. Stand firm here, if you

---

"This is the glad tidings, that we are made righteous by Christ. It is not a righteousness wrought by us, but given to us, and put upon us. This carnal reason cannot comprehend, and being proud rejects and argues against it. How can this thing be? But faith closes with it and rejoices in it. Without either doing or suffering, the sinner is acquitted and justified, and stands as guiltless of breach as having fulfilled the whole law."—*Archbishop Leighton.* 1670.

"Christ is now the righteousness of all them that truly do believe in Him. He for them paid their ransom by His death. He for them fulfilled the law in His life. So that now in Him and by Him every true Christian man may be called a fulfiller of the law; forasmuch as that which their infirmity lacked, Christ's justice has supplied."—*Homily on Salvation written by Archbishop Cranmer.* 1547.

"This is the call of the Gospel, He that dares trust Christ with His soul upon the warrant of the Gospel shall be saved forever. The Lord tries people this way. We have no more to do but take pen in hand, and say Amen, O Lord: it is a good bargain and a true word, and I will trust my soul on it. This is believing."—*Traill.* 1690.

value your soul's peace. I see many walking in darkness, and having no light, from confused notions as to what faith is. They hear that saving faith will work by love, and produce holiness; and not finding all this at once in themselves, they think they have no faith at all. They forget that these things are the fruits of faith, and not faith itself, and that to doubt whether we have faith because we do not see them at once, is like doubting whether a tree be alive, because it does not bear fruit the very day we plant it in the ground. I charge you to settle it firmly in your mind that in the matter of your forgiveness and justification there is but one thing required, and that is simple faith in Christ.[22]

I know well that the natural heart dislikes this doctrine. It runs counter to man's notions of religion. It leaves him no room to boast. Man's idea is to come to Christ with a price in his hand,—his regularity, his morality, his repentance, his goodness,—and so, as it were, to buy his pardon and justification. The Spirit's teaching is quite different; it is first of all to believe. "Whosoever *believeth* shall not perish." (John iii. 16.)

Some say, such doctrine cannot be right, because it makes the way to heaven too easy. I fear that many such persons, if the truth were spoken, find it too hard. I believe in reality it is easier to give a fortune in building a cathedral like York Minster, or to go to the stake

---

22 "St. Paul declareth nothing on the behalf of man concerning his justification, but only a true and lively faith; which nevertheless is the gift of God, and not man's only work without God. And yet that faith doth not shut out repentance, hope, love, dread, and the fear of God, to be joined with faith in every man that is justified: but it shutteth them out from the office of justifying."— *Homily on Salvation, by Archbishop Cranmer.* 1547.

"How is the great benefit of justification applied to me, and apprehended by us? This is done on our part by faith alone, and that not considered as a virtue inherent in us working by love; but only as an instrument or hand of the soul stretched forth to lay hold on the Lord our righteousness."—*Archbishop Usher.* 1670.

and be burned, than thoroughly to receive justification by faith without the deeds of the law, and to enter heaven as a sinner saved by grace.[23]

Some say this doctrine is foolishness and enthusiasm. I answer, this is just what was said of it 1800 years ago, and is a vain cavil now, as it was then. So far from the charge being true, a thousand facts can prove this doctrine to be from God. No doctrine certainly has produced such mighty effects in the world, as the simple proclamation of free forgiveness through faith in Christ.

This is the glorious doctrine that was the strength of the apostles when they went forth to the Gentiles to preach a new religion. They began a few poor fishermen in a despised corner of the earth. They turned the world upside down. They changed the face of the Roman empire. They emptied the heathen temples of their worshippers, and made the whole system of idolatry crumble away. And what was the weapon by which they did it all? It was *free forgiveness through faith in Jesus Christ*.

This is the doctrine which brought light into Europe 300 years ago, at the time of the blessed Reformation, and enabled one solitary monk, Martin Luther, to shake the whole church of Rome. Through his preaching and writing the scales fell from men's eyes, and the chains of their souls were loosed. And what was the lever that gave him his power? It was *free forgiveness through faith in Jesus Christ*.

This is the doctrine that revived our own church in the middle of the last century, when Whitefield and the Wesleys, and Romaine, and Berridge, and Venn broke

---

[23] "It is as truly as commonly said, that such as think believing easy, know not what believing is." — *Traill*. 1690.

"It is harder to believe in Christ for righteonsness than to keep all the commandments, because keeping the commandments hath something in the heart of man agreeing with it, but so hath not the way of justification by faith." — *Philip Henry's Sermons*. 1690.

the wretched spirit of slumber that had come over the land, and roused men to think. They began a mighty work, with little seeming likelihood of success. They began, few in number, with small encouragement from the rich and great. But they prospered. And why?—Because they preached *free forgiveness through faith in Christ*.

This is the doctrine which is the true strength of any church on earth at this day. It is not orders, or endowments, or liturgies, or learning, that will keep a church alive. Let free forgiveness through Christ be faithfully proclaimed in her pulpits, and the gates of hell shall not prevail against her. Let it be buried or kept back, and her candlestick shall soon be taken away. When the Saracens invaded the lands where Jerome and Athanasius, Cyprian and Augustine, once wrote and preached, they found bishops and liturgies, I make no question. But I fear they found no preaching of free forgiveness of sins, and so they swept the churches of those lands clean away. They were a body without a vital principle, and therefore they fell. Let us never forget the brightest days of a church are those *when Christ crucified is most exalted*. The dens and caves of the earth where the early Christians met to hear of the love of Jesus, were more full of glory and beauty in God's sight than ever was St. Peter's at Rome. The meanest barn at this day, where the true way of pardon is offered to sinners, is a far more honorable place than is the cathedral of Cologne or Milan. A church is only useful so far as she exalts *free forgiveness through Christ*.

This is the doctrine which of all others is the mightiest engine for pulling down the kingdom of Satan. The Greenlanders were unmoved, so long as the Moravians told them of the creation and the fall of man; but when they heard of redeeming love, their frozen hearts melted like snow in spring. Preach salvation by the sacraments, exalt the church above Christ, and keep back the doctrine of the atonement, and the devil cares little,—his goods are at peace. But preach a full Christ and a free pardon, and then Satan will have great wrath, for he knows he has but a short time. John Berridge said he went on preaching morality and nothing else, till he found there was not a moral man in his parish. But when he changed his plan, and began to preach the love of Christ to sinners, then there was a stirring of the dry bones, and a mighty turning to God.

This is the only doctrine which will ever bring peace to an uneasy conscience, and rest to a troubled soul. A man may get on pretty well without it so long as he is asleep about his spiritual condition. But once let him awake from his slumber, and nothing will ever calm him but the blood of atonement and the peace of Christ.[24] How any one can undertake to be a minister of religion without a firm grasp of this doctrine, I never can understand. For myself, I can only say, I should think my office a most painful one, if I had not the message of free forgiveness to convey. It would be miserable work indeed to visit the sick and dying, if I could not say, "Behold the Lamb of God,—believe on the Lord Jesus Christ, and thou shalt be saved." The right hand of a Christian minister is the doctrine of free forgiveness through faith in Christ. Give us this doctrine, and we have power: we will never despair of doing good to men's souls. Take away this doctrine, and we are weak as water. We may read the prayers, and go

---

24 "Man's conscience can never rest nor be at peace, until it be settled in the full persuasion of remission of sins in the death and resurrection of Jesus Christ; whereby God receiveth us into His favor, and is at one with us through Him."—*Archbishop Sandys.* 1585.

See also a most interesting account of the effect produced on Luther, when in great distress of soul, by the words, "I believe in the forgiveness of sins," repeated to him by an aged monk.—*D'Aubigne's History of the Reformation.* One vol. edition, page 68.

through a round of forms, but we are like Samson with his hair shorn, our strength is gone. Souls will not be benefited by us, and good will not be done.

Reader, I commend the things I have been saying to your notice. I am not ashamed of free pardon through faith in Christ, whatever some may say against the doctrine. I am not ashamed of it, for its fruits speak for themselves. It has done things that no other doctrine can do. It has effected moral changes which laws and punishments have failed to work,—which magistrates and policemen have labored after in vain, which mechanics' institutes and secular knowledge have proved utterly powerless to produce. Just as the fiercest lunatics in Bethlehem Hospital became suddenly gentle when kindly treated, even so the worst and most hardened sinners have often become as little children, when told of Jesus loving them and willing to forgive. I can well understand Paul ending his Epistle to the erring Galatians with that solemn burst of feeling, "God forbid that I should glory save in the cross of our Lord Jesus Christ. (Gal. vi. 14.) The crown has indeed fallen from a Christian's head, when he leaves the doctrine of justification by faith.

See now how you should ask yourself whether you have really received the truth which I have been dwelling on, and know it by experience. Jesus, and faith in Him, is the only way to the Father. He that thinks to climb into paradise by some other road, will find himself fearfully mistaken. Other foundation can no man lay for an immortal soul than that of which I have been feebly speaking. He that ventures himself here is safe. He that is off this rock has got no standing ground at all.

See too how you should seriously consider what kind of a ministry you are in the habit of attending, supposing you have a choice. You have reason indeed to be careful. It is not *all the same* where you go, whatever people may say. There are many places of worship, I fear, where you might look long for Christ crucified, and never find Him. He is buried under outward ceremonies,—thrust behind the baptismal font,—lost sight of under the shadow of the church. "They have taken away my Lord, and I know not where they have laid Him." Take heed where you settle yourself. Try all by this single test, "Is Jesus and free forgiveness proclaimed here?" There may be comfortable pews—there may be good singing,—there may be learned sermons. But if Christ's Gospel is not the sun and centre of the whole place, do not continue there. Say rather with Isaac, "Here is the wood and the fire, but where is the Lamb?" Be very sure this is not the place for your soul.

Reader, remember these things, and you will be wise. I have set before you the way of life. I have told you where pardon is to be found. O beware lest an offer being made you of free forgiveness, any of you should come short of it.

III. *Let me, in the third place, encourage all who wish to be forgiven.*

I dare be sure this paper will be read by some one who feels he is not yet a forgiven soul. My heart's desire and prayer is, that such an one may seek his pardon at once. And I would fain help him forward, by showing him the kind of forgiveness offered to him, and the glorious privileges within his reach.

Listen to me then, while I try to exhibit to you the treasures of Gospel forgiveness. I cannot describe its fulness as I ought. Its riches are indeed unsearchable. (Ephes. iii. 8.) But if you turn away from it, you shall not be able to say in the day of judgment, you did not at all know what it was.

Consider then for one thing, that the forgiveness set before you is a *great and broad forgiveness*. Hear what the Prince of Peace Himself declares, "All sins shall be forgiven unto the sons of men, and blasphemies where-with-soever they shall blaspheme." (Mark iii. 28.) "Though your sins be as scarlet, they shall become white as snow; though they be red like crimson, they shall be as wool." (Isaiah i. 18.) Yes! though your trespasses be more in number than the hairs of your head, the stars in heaven, the leaves of the forest, the blades of grass, the grains of sand on the seashore, still they can be all pardoned. As the waters of Noah's flood covered over and hid the tops of the highest hills, so can the blood of Jesus cover over and hide your mightiest sins. "His blood cleanseth from all sin." (1 John i. 7.) Though to you they seem written with the point of a diamond, they can all be effaced from the book of God's remembrance by that precious blood. Paul names a long list of abominations which the Corinthians had committed, and then says, "such were some of you, but ye are washed." (1 Cor. vi. 11.)

Furthermore, it is a *full and complete forgiveness*. It is not like David's pardon to Absalom,—a permission to return home, but not a full restoration to favor. (2 Sam. xiv. 24.) It is not, as some fancy, a mere letting off, and letting alone. It is a pardon so complete, that he who has it is reckoned as righteous as if he had never sinned at all.[25] His iniquities are blotted out. They are removed from him as far as the east and the west. (Psalm ciii. 12.) There remains no condemnation for him. The Father sees him joined to Christ, and is well pleased. The Son beholds him clothed with His own righteousness, and says, "Thou art all fair, there is no spot in thee." (Cant. iv. 7.) Blessed be God that it is so. I verily believe if the

---

25 "It is not therefore, O soul, a mere negative mercy that God intends thee in the pardon of thy sins: it is not merely the removing of the curse and wrath which thy sins have deserved, though that alone can never be sufficiently admired. But the same hand that plucks thee out of hell by pardoning grace and mercy, lifts thee up to heaven by what it gives thee together with thy pardon, even a right and title to the glorious inheritance of saints above."—*Bishop Hopkins.* 1680.

best of us all had only one blot left for himself to wipe out, he would miss eternal life. If the holiest child of Adam were in heaven all but his little finger, and to get in depended on himself, I am sure he would never enter the kingdom. If Noah, Daniel, and Job, had had but one day's sins to wash away, they would never have been saved. Praised be God that in the matter of our pardon there is nothing left for man to do. Jesus does all, and man has only to hold out an empty hand and receive.

Furthermore, it is a *free and unconditional forgiveness*. It is not burdened with an "if," like Solomon's pardon to Adonijah, "If he will show himself a worthy man." (1 Kings i. 52.) Nor yet are you obliged to carry a price in your hand, or bring a character with you to prove yourself deserving of mercy. Jesus requires but one character, and that is, that you should feel yourself a sinful bad man. He invites you to "buy wine and milk without money and without price," and declares, "Whosoever will, let him take the water of life freely." (Isaiah lv. 1.; Rev. xxii. 17.) Like David in the cave of Adullam, He receives "every one that feels in distress and a debtor," and rejects none. (1 Sam. xxii. 2.) Are you a sinner? Do you want a Saviour? Then come to Jesus, just as you are, and your soul shall live.

Again, it is an *offered forgiveness*. I have read of earthly kings who knew not how to show mercy,—of Henry the Eighth of England, who spared neither man nor woman; of James the Fifth of Scotland, who would never show favor to a Douglas. The King of kings is not like them. He calls on man to come to Him and be pardoned. "Unto you, O men, I call, and my voice is to the sons of men." (Prov. viii. 4.) "Ho, every one that thirsteth, come ye to the waters." (Isaiah lv. 1.) "If any man thirst, let him come unto me and drink." (John vii. 37.) "Come unto me, all ye that labor and are heavy-laden, and I will give you rest." (Matt. xi. 28.) O Reader, it ought to be a great comfort to you and me to hear of any pardon at all; but to hear Jesus Himself inviting us, to see Jesus Himself holding out his hand to us,—the Saviour seeking the sinner before the sinner seeks the Saviour,—this is encouragement, this is strong consolation indeed.

Again, it is a *willing forgiveness*. I have heard of pardons granted in reply to long entreaty, and wrung out by much importunity. King Edward the Third of England would not spare the citizens of Calais till they came to him with halters round their necks, and his own queen interceded for them on her knees. But Jesus is "good and ready to forgive." (Psalm lxxxvi. 5.) He delighteth in mercy. (Micah vii. 18.) Judgment is his strange work. He is not willing that any should perish. (2 Peter iii. 9.) He would fain have all men saved, and come to the knowledge of the truth. (1 Tim. ii. 4.) He wept over unbelieving Jerusalem. "As I live," He says, "I have no pleasure in the death of the wicked. Turn ye, turn ye, from your evil ways: why will ye die?" (Ezek. xxxiii. 11.) Ah! Reader, you and I may well come boldly to the throne of grace. He who sits there is far more willing and ready to give mercy than you and I to receive it.

Beside this, it is a *tried forgiveness*. Thousands and tens of thousands have sought for pardon at the mercy-seat of Christ, and not one has ever returned to say that he sought in vain. Sinners of every name and nation,—sinners of every sort and description, have knocked at the door of the fold, and none have ever been refused admission. Zacchæus the extortioner, Magdalen the harlot, Saul the persecutor, Peter the denier of his Lord, the Jews who crucified the Prince of life, the idolatrous Athenians, the adulterous Corinthians, the ignorant Africans, the blood-thirsty New Zealanders,—all have ventured their souls on Christ's promises of pardon, and none have ever found them fail. Ah! Reader, if the way I set before you were a new and untravelled way, you might well feel faint-hearted. But it is not so. It is an old path. It is a path worn by the feet of many pilgrims, and a path in which the footsteps are all one way. The treasury of Christ's mercies has never been found empty. The well of living waters has never proved dry.

Beside this, it is a *present forgiveness*. All that believe in Jesus are at once justified from all things. (Acts xiii. 38.) The very day the younger son returned to his father's house, he was clothed with the best robe, had the ring put on his hand and the shoes on his feet. (Luke 15.) The very day Zacchæus received Jesus he heard those comfortable words, "This day is salvation come to this house." (Luke xix. 9.) The very day that David said, "I have sinned against the Lord," he was told by Nathan, "The Lord also hath put away thy sin." (2 Sam. xii. 13.) The very day you first flee to Christ your sins are all removed. Your pardon is not a thing far away, to be obtained only by hard work, and after many years. It is nigh at hand. It is close to you, within your reach, all ready to be bestowed. Believe, and that very moment it is your own. "He that believeth is not condemned." (John iii. 18.) It is not said, "He shall not be," or "will not be," but *"is not."* From the time of his believing condemnation is gone. "He that believeth hath everlasting life." (John iii. 36.) It is not said, "He shall have," or "will have," it is *"hath."* It is his own as surely as if he was in heaven, though not so evidently so to his own eyes. Ah! Reader, you must not think forgiveness will be nearer to a believer in the day of judgment than it was in the hour he first believed. His complete salvation from the *power* of sin is every year nearer and nearer to him, but as to his forgiveness and justification, it is a finished work from the very minute he first commits himself to Christ.

Last, and best of all, it is an *everlasting forgiveness*. It is not like Shimei's pardon, a pardon that may some time be revoked and taken away. (1 Kings ii. 9.) Once justified, you are justified forever. Once written down in the book of life, your name shall never be blotted out. The sins of God's children are said to be cast into the depths of the sea,—to be sought for and not found,—to be remembered no more,—to be cast behind God's back. (Mic. vii. 19. Jerem. l. 20, xxxi. 34. Isaiah xxxviii. 17.) Some people fancy they may be justified one year, and condemned another,—children of adoption at one time, and strangers by-and-by,—heirs of the kingdom in the beginning of their days, and yet servants of the devil in their end. I cannot find this in the Bible;—as the New Zealander told the Romish priest, I do not see it in the book. It seems to me to overturn the good news of the Gospel altogether, and to tear up its comforts by the roots. I believe the salvation Jesus offers is an everlasting salvation, and a pardon once sealed with His blood shall never be reversed.

Reader, I have set before you the nature of the forgiveness offered to you. I have told you but a little of it, for my words are weaker than my will. The half of it remains untold. The greatness of it is far more than any report of mine.[26] But I think I have said enough to show you it is worth the seeking, and I can wish you nothing better than that you may strive to make it your own.

Do you call it nothing to look forward to death without fear, and to judgment without doubtings, and to eternity without a sinking heart? Do you call it nothing to feel the world slipping from your grasp, and to see the grave getting ready for you, and the valley of the shadow of death opening before your eyes, and yet not be afraid? Do you call it nothing to be able to think

---

26 Who is a God like unto thee? None can pardon as thou dost. None can pardon so freely,—none so fully,—none so continually,—none so eternally,—none so indifferently,—whether in respect of sinners or sin, as thou dost. It is all one to thee what the sins are, and all one to thee whose the sins are, so they come to ask thy pardon."—*Joseph Caryl*. 1670.

of the great day of account, the throne, the books, the Judge, the assembled worlds, the revealing of secrets, the final sentence, and yet to feel, "I am safe?" This is the portion, and this the privilege of a forgiven soul.

Such an one is *on a rock*. When the rain of God's wrath descends, and the floods come, and the winds blow, his feet shall not slide, his habitation shall be sure.

Such an one is *in an ark*. When the last fiery deluge is sweeping over all things on the surface of the earth, it shall not come nigh him. He shall be caught up and borne securely above it all.

Such an one is *in a hiding place*. When God arises to judge terribly the earth, and men are calling to rocks and mountains to fall upon them and cover them, the everlasting arms shall be thrown around him, and the storm shall pass over his head. He shall abide under the shadow of the Almighty.

Such an one is in *a city of refuge*. The accuser of the brethren can lay no charge against him. The law cannot condemn him. There is a wall between him and the avenger of blood. The enemies of his soul cannot hurt him. He is in a secure sanctuary.

Such an one is *rich*. He has treasure in heaven which cannot be affected by worldly changes, compared to which Peru and California are nothing at all. He need not envy the richest merchants and bankers. He has a portion that will endure when bank-notes and sovereigns are worthless things. He can say like the Spanish ambassador, when shown the treasury at Venice, "My master's treasury has no bottom."[27] He has Christ.

Such an one is *insured*. He is ready for anything that may happen. Nothing can harm him. Banks may break, and governments may be overturned. Famine and pestilence may rage around him. Sickness and

---

27 This was said boastfully, at a time when the gold mines of Mexico and South America formed part of the possessions of the Spanish crown.

sorrow may visit his own fireside. But still he is ready, for all,—ready for health, ready for disease,—ready for tears, ready for joy,—ready for poverty, ready for plenty,—ready for life, ready for death. He has Christ. He is a pardoned soul. "Blessed" indeed "is he whose transgression is forgiven, and whose sin is covered." Psalm xxxii. 1.)[28]

Reader, how will you escape if you neglect so great salvation? Why should you not lay hold on it at once, and say, Pardon me, even me also, O my Saviour. What would you have, if the way I have set before you does not satisfy you? Come while the door is open. Ask, and you shall receive.

IV. *Let me give you, in the last place, some marks of having found forgiveness.*

I dare not leave out this point. Too many persons presume they are forgiven, who have no evidences to show. Not a few cannot think it possible they are forgiven, who are plainly in the way to heaven, though they may not see it themselves. I would fain raise hope

---

28 "If we have Christ, then have we with Him and by Him, all good things whatsoever we can in our hearts wish or desire,—as victory over death, sin, and hell; we have the favor of God, peace with Him, holiness, wisdom, justice, power, life, and redemption; we have by Him perpetual health, wealth, joy, and bliss everlasting."—*Church of England Homily of the fear of death.* 1547.

"He that hath got a view of Christ, and reads his own pardon in Christ's sufferings, can rejoice in this in the midst of all other sufferings, and look on death without apprehension, yea with gladness,—for the sting is out. Christ hath made all pleasant to him by this one thing, that He suffered once for sins. Christ hath perfumed the cross and the grave, and made all sweet. The pardoned man finds himself light, skips, and leaps, and through Christ strengthening him can encounter any troubles, yea he can submit patiently to the Lord in any correction. Thou hast forgiven my sin, therefore deal with me as thou wilt: all is well."—*Archbishop Leighton.* 1670.

"A believer is a rich man and an honorable, even if he be a beggar on the dunghill. Christ cannot be poor, and he is a fellow-heir with Christ."—*Rutherford's Christ Dying.* 1647.

in some, and self-inquiry in others; and to do this, let me tell you the leading marks of a forgiven soul.

Forgiven souls *hate sin*. They can enter most fully into the words of our Communion Service, "the remembrance of sin is grievous unto them, and the burden of it is intolerable." It is the serpent which bit them: how should they not shrink from it with horror? It is the poison which brought them to the brink of eternal death: how should they not loathe it with a Godly disgust? It is the Egyptian enemy which kept them in hard bondage: how should not the very memory of it be bitter to their hearts? It is the disease of which they carry the marks and scars about them, and from which they scarcely recovered: well may they dread it, flee from it, and long to be delivered altogether from its power. Remember how the woman in Simon's house wept over the feet of Jesus. (Luke vii. 38.) Remember how the Ephesians publicly burned their wicked books. (Acts xix. 19.) Remember how Paul mourned over his youthful transgressions, "I am not meet to be called an apostle, because I persecuted the church of God." (1 Cor. xv. 9.) Ah! Reader, if you and sin are friends, you and God are not yet reconciled. You are not meet for heaven, for one main part of heaven's excellence is the absence of all sin.[29]

---

29 "If thou have no mind to leave sin, and sin grieveth thee not, and thou art content to go forward in the same, and thou delightest in it, and hatest it not, neither feelest what sin is;—when thou art in such a case, then thou hast no faith, and therefore art like to perish everlastingly."—*Bishop Latimer*, 1547.

"The real Christian is an avowed enemy of sin. Shall I ever be friends with that, says he, which killed my Lord? No, but I will even kill it, and do it by applying His death. The true penitent is sworn to be the death of sin. He may be surprised by it, but there is no possibility of reconcilement between them. Thou that livest kindly and familiarly with sin, and either openly declarest thyself for it, or hast a secret love to it, where canst thou reap any comfort?—Not from Christ's sufferings."—*Archbishop Leighton*. 1670.

Forgiven souls *love Christ*. This is that one thing they can say, if they dare say nothing else,—they do love Christ. His person, His office, His work, His name, His cross, His blood, His words, His example, His day, His ordinances, all, all are precious to forgiven souls. The ministry which exalts Him most, is that which they enjoy most. The Books which are most full of Him, are most pleasant to their minds. The people on earth they feel most drawn to, are those in whom they see something of Christ. His name is as ointment poured forth, and comes with a peculiar sweetness to their ears. (Cant. i. 3.) They would tell you they cannot help feeling as they do. He is their Redeemer, their Shepherd, their Physician, their King, their strong Deliverer, their gracious Guide, their hope, their joy, their all. Were it not for Him they would be of all men most miserable. They would as soon consent that you should take the sun out of the sky, as Christ out of their religion. Those people who talk of "the Lord," and "the almighty," and "the Deity," and so forth, but have not a word to say about Christ, are in anything but a right state of mind. What saith the Scripture? "He that honoreth not the Son, honoreth not the Father which hath sent Him." (John v. 23.)[30] "If any man love not the Lord Jesus Christ, let him be anathema." (1 Cor. xvi. 22.)

Forgiven souls *are humble*. They cannot forget that they owe all they have and hope for to free grace, and this keeps them lowly. They are brands plucked from the fire,—debtors who could not pay for themselves,—captives who must have have remained in prison forever, but for undeserved mercy,—wandering sheep who were ready to perish when the Shepherd found them,—and what right then have they to be proud? I do not deny that there are proud saints. But this I do say, they

---

30 "He that lifts not up Christ above all hath no interest in Christ at all. He that sets not Christ above all is not a disciple of Christ."— *Thomas Brooks*. 1660.

are of all God's creatures the most inconsistent, — and of all God's children, the most likely to stumble and pierce themselves with many sorrows. Forgiveness more often produces the spirit of Jacob: — "I am not worthy of the least of all the mercies, and of all the truth which thou hast showed unto thy servant." (Gen. xxxii. 10); and of Hezekiah, "I shall go softly all my years" (Isaiah xxxviii. 15); and of the apostle Paul, "I am less than the least of all saints, — chief of sinners." (Ephes. iii. 8; — 1 Tim. i. 15.) Reader, when you and I have nothing we can call our own but sin and weakness, there is surely no garment that becomes us so well as humility.

Forgiven souls *are holy*. Their chief desire is to please Him who has saved them, to do His will, to glorify Him 'in body and in spirit, which are His. "What shall I render unto the Lord for all His benefits," is a leading principle in a pardoned heart. It was the remembrance of Jesus showing mercy that made Paul in labors so abundant, and in doing good so unwearied. It was a sense of pardon that made Zacchæus say, "The half of my goods I give to the poor, and if I have taken anything from any man by false accusation, I restore him fourfold." (Luke xix. 8.) Reader, if you point out to me believers who are in a carnal, slothful state of soul, I reply in the words of Peter, "They have forgotten they were purged from their old sins." (2 Peter i. 9.) But if you show me a man deliberately living an unholy and licentious life, and yet boasting that his sins are forgiven, I answer he is under a ruinous delusion, and is not forgiven at all. I would not believe he is forgiven, if an angel from heaven affirmed it, and I charge you not to believe it too. Pardon of sin and love of sin are like oil and water, they will never go together. All that are washed in the blood of Christ, are also sanctified by the spirit of Christ.[31]

---

31 "Are you in a willing league with any known sin? Yea, would you willingly, if you might be saved in that way, give up your-

Forgiven souls *are forgiving*. They do as they have been done by. They look over the offences of their brethren. They endeavor to walk in love, as Christ loved them, and gave Himself for them. They remember how God for Christ's sake forgave them, and endeavor to do the same toward their fellow-creatures. Has He forgiven them pounds, and shall they not forgive a few pence? Doubtless in this, as in everything else, they come short;—but this is their desire and their aim. A spiteful, quarrelsome Christian is a scandal to his profession. It is very hard to believe that such an one has ever sat at the foot of the cross, has ever considered how he is praying against himself every time he uses the Lord's prayer, and saying as it were, "Father, do not forgive me my trespasses at all." But it is still harder to understand what such an one would do in heaven, if he got there. All ideas of heaven in which forgiveness has not a place, are castles in the air, and vain fancies. Forgiveness is the way by which every saved soul enters heaven. Forgiveness is the only title by which he remains in heaven. Forgiveness is the eternal subject of song with all the redeemed who inhabit heaven. Surely an unforgiving soul in heaven would find his heart completely out of tune. Surely we know nothing of Christ's love to us but the name of it, if we do not love our brethren.

Reader, I lay these things before you. I know well there are great diversities in the degree of men's attainments in grace, and that saving faith in Christ is consistent with many imperfections. But still I do believe the marks I have just been naming will generally be found more or less in all forgiven souls.

I cannot conceal from you these marks should raise in many minds great searchings of heart. I must be

---

self to voluptuousness and ungodliness, and not at all desire to follow Jesus Christ in the way of holiness? Then, truly I have not anything to say for your comfort." —*Archbishop Leighton*. 1670.

plain. I fear there are thousands of persons called Christians who know nothing of these marks. They are baptized. They keep their church. They would not on any account be reckoned infidels. But as to true repentance, and saving faith, union with Christ, and sanctification of the Spirit, they are names and words of which they know nothing at all.

Now if this paper is read by such persons, it will probably either alarm them, or make them very angry. If it makes them angry, I shall be sorry. If it alarms them, I shall be glad. *I want to alarm them.* I want to awaken them from their present state. I want them to take in the great fact, that they are not yet forgiven, they have not peace with God, and are on the high-road to destruction.

I must say this, for I see no alternative. It seems neither Christian faithfulness, nor Christian charity, to keep it back. I see certain marks of pardoned souls laid down in Scripture. I see an utter want of these marks in many men and women around me. How then can I avoid the conclusion that they are not yet forgiven? And how shall I do the work of a faithful watchman, if I do not write it down plainly in so many words? Where is the use of crying peace, peace, when there is no peace? Where is the honesty of acting the part of a lying physician, and telling people there is no danger, when in reality they are fast drawing near to eternal death? Surely the blood of souls would be required at my hands, if I wrote to you anything less than the truth. "If the trumpet give an uncertain sound, who shall prepare himself for the battle."

Examine yourselves then, before this subject is forgotten. Consider of what sort your religion is. Try it by the marks I have just set before you. I have endeavored to make them as broad and general as I can, for fear of causing any heart to be sad that God has not made sad. If you know anything of them, though it be but a little, I am thankful, and entreat you to go forward. But if you know nothing of them in your own experience, let me say in all affection, I stand in doubt of you. I tremble for your soul.

1. And now, before I conclude, let me put a home *question* to every one who reads this paper. It shall be short and plain, but it is all-important,—"*Are you forgiven?*"

I have told you all I can about forgiveness. Your need of forgiveness,—the way of forgiveness,—the encouragements to seek forgiveness,—the marks of having found it,—all have been placed before you. Bring the whole subject before your own heart, and ask yourself, "Am I forgiven? Either I am, or I am not. Which of the two is it?"

You believe, perhaps, there is forgiveness of sins. You believe that Christ died for sinners, and that He offers a pardon to the most ungodly. But are you forgiven *yourself*? Have you yourself laid hold on Christ by faith, and found peace through His blood? What profit is there to you in forgiveness, except you get the benefit of it? What does it profit the shipwrecked sailor, that the life-boat is alongside, if he sticks by the wreck, and does not jump in and escape? What does it avail the sick man, that the doctor offers him a medicine, if he only looks at it and does not swallow it? Except you lay hold of your own soul, you will be as surely lost as if there was no forgiveness at all.[32]

---

32 "This sweet truth, that Christ died for sinners, and rose again for their justification, will not help thee, unless thou hope for thyself; yea, thou wilt remain in thy old skin, while using this blessed saying, as a cover for thy sins. Do not take this consolation; for although He died for all and rose again, yet, to thee He is not risen, for thou hast not yet apprehended by faith His resurrection; the words thou hast heard, but their power thou hast not experienced."—*Martin Luther*.

"This is it which bringeth comfort unto the wounded soul and afflicted conscience,—not that Christ is a Saviour, for what am I the better for that?—but a Saviour unto me. What is it to

Reader, if ever your sins are to be forgiven, it must be now,—now in this life, if ever in the life to come,—now in this world, if they are to be found blotted out when Jesus comes again. There must be actual business between you and Christ. Your sins must be laid on Him by faith. His righteousness must be laid on you. His blood must be applied to your conscience, or else your sins will meet you in the day of judgment, and sink you into hell. Oh! Reader, how can you trifle when such things are at stake? How can you be content to leave it uncertain whether you are forgiven? Surely that a man can make his will, insure his life, give directions about his funeral, and yet leave his soul's affairs in uncertainty, is a wonderful thing indeed.

2. Let me next give a *solemn warning* to every one who reads this paper, and knows in his conscience he is not forgiven.

Your soul is in awful danger. You may die this year. And if you die as you are, you are lost forever. If you die without pardon, without pardon you will rise again at the last day. There is a sword over your head that hangs by a single hair. There is but a step between you and death. Oh! I wonder that you can sleep quietly in your bed.

You are *not yet forgiven*. Then what have you got by your religion? You go to church. You have a Bible, you have a prayer-book, and perhaps a hymn-book. You hear sermons. You join in services. It may be you go to the Lord's table. But what have you really *got* after all? Any hope? Any peace? Any joy? Any comfort? Noth-

---

my belly that bread is prepared for others, unless I be assured that my part is therein? What is it to my soul that Christ died for others, unless I know that my sins are washed away in His blood? It may be good for Moses, or Paul, or Peter, or James, or Stephen, but what is it unto me? It is "mine" and "thine," as Luther did well teach; it is "my" God and "thy" Saviour, which doth satisfy thirsty consciences."—*George Abbott, Archbishop of Canterbury*. 1612.

ing, literally nothing! You have got nothing but mere temporal things, if you are not a pardoned soul.

You are *not yet forgiven*. But you trust God will be merciful. And why should He be merciful, if you will not seek Him in His own appointed way? Merciful He doubtless is, wonderfully merciful to all who come to Him in the name of Jesus. But if you choose to despise His directions, and make a road to heaven of your own, you will find to your cost there is no mercy for you.

You are *not yet forgiven*. But you hope you shall be some day. I cannot away with that expression. It is like thrusting off the hand of conscience, and seizing it by the throat to stop its voice. Why are you more likely to seek forgiveness at a future time? Why should you not seek it now? Now is the time for gathering the bread of life. The day of the Lord is fast drawing near, and then no man can work. (Exod. xvi. 26.) The seventh trumpet will soon sound. The kingdoms of this world will soon become the kingdoms of our God and of His Christ. Woe to the house which is found without the scarlet line, and without the mark of blood upon the door! (Josh. ii. 18. Exod. xii. 13.)

Well! you may not feel your need of forgiveness now. But a time may come when you will want it. The Lord in mercy grant that it may not then be too late.[33]

3. Let me next give an *earnest invitation* to all who read this paper, and desire forgiveness.

I know not what you are, or what you may have been in time past, but I say boldly, Come to Christ by faith, and you shall have a pardon. High or low, rich or poor, young men and maidens, old men and children,—you cannot be worse than Manasseh and Paul before conversion, than David and Peter after conver-

---

33 "Those poor who are without a covering for their bodies are to be pitied; but with what tears should we lament those,—how rich soever they are in this world,—who are without a covering for their souls, and so stand naked in the storm, and under the dreadful droppings of the wrath of God."—*Joseph Caryl*. 1650.

sion,—come all of you to Christ, and you shall be freely forgiven.

Think not for a moment that you have some great thing to do before you come to Christ. Such a notion is of the earth, earthy; the Gospel bids you come just as you are. Man's idea is to make his peace with God by repentance, and then come to Christ at last: the Gospel way is to receive peace from Christ first of all, and begin with Him. Man's idea is to amend and turn over a new leaf, and so work his way up to reconciliation and friendship with God: the Gospel way is first to be friends with God through Christ, and then to work. Man's idea is to toil up the hill, and find life *at the top:* the Gospel way is first to live by faith in Christ, and then to do His will.

And judge ye, every one, judge ye which is true Christianity? Which is the good news? Which is the glad tidings? First the fruits of the Spirit, and then peace; or first peace, and then the fruit of the Spirit? First sanctification, and then pardon; or first pardon, and then sanctification? First service, and then life; or first life, and then service? Reader, your own heart can well supply the answer.

Come then, willing to receive, and not thinking how much you can bring. Come, willing to take what Christ offers, and not fancying you can give anything in return. Come with your sins, and no other qualification but a hearty desire for pardon, and so sure as the Bible is true you shall be saved.

You may tell me you are not worthy, you are not good enough, you are not elect. I answer, you are a sinner, and you want to be saved, and what more do you want? You are one of those whom Jesus came to save. Come to Him, and you shall have life.[34] Take with you

---

34 "The longer thou dost live without Christ, the more grains dost thou collect to make the mountain of thy sins higher."—*Martin Luther.*

words, and He will hear you graciously. Tell Him all your soul's necessities, and I know He will give heed. Tell Him you have heard He receiveth sinners, and that you are such. Tell Him you have heard He has the keys of life in His hand, and entreat Him to let you in. Tell Him you come in dependence on His own promises, and ask Him to fulfil His word, and do as He has said. Do this in simplicity and sincerity, and, my soul for yours, you shall not ask in vain. Do this, and you shall find Him faithful and just to forgive your sins, and to cleanse you from all unrighteousness.

4. Last of all, let me give a *word of exhortation* to all forgiven souls.

You are forgiven. Then know the full extent of your privileges, and learn to rejoice in the Lord. You and I are great sinners, but then we have a great Saviour. You and I have sinned sins that are past man's knowledge, but then we have the love of Christ, which passeth knowledge, to rest upon. You and I feel our hearts to be a bubbling fountain of evil, but then we have another fountain of greater power, even Christ's blood, to which we may daily resort. You and I have mighty enemies to contend with, but then the Captain of our salvation is mightier still, and is ever with us. Why should our hearts be troubled? Why should we be disquieted and cast down? O men of little faith that we are! Wherefore do we doubt?[35]

Let us strive every year to grow in grace, and in the knowledge of our Lord Jesus Christ. It is sad to be content with a little religion. It is honorable to covet the best gifts. We ought not to be satisfied with the same kind of hearing, and reading, and praying which satisfied us in years gone by. We ought to labor every year to

---

35 "A great many believers walk upon the promises at God's call in the way to heaven even as a child upon weak ice, which they are afraid will crack under them, and leave them in the depth."— *Traill*. 1690.

throw more heart and reality into everything we do in our religion. To love Christ more intensely,—to abhor evil more thoroughly,—to cleave to what is good more closely,—to watch even our least ways more narrowly,—to declare very plainly that we seek a country,—to put on the Lord Jesus Christ, and be clothed with Him in every place and company,—to see more,—to feel more,—to know more,—to do more,—to pray more;—these ought to be our aims and desires, every year we begin. Truly there is room for improvement in us all.[36]

Let us try to do good to the souls of others more than we have done hitherto. Alas! it is poor work indeed to be swallowed up in our own spiritual concerns, and taken up with our own spiritual ailments, and never to think of others. We forget that there is such a thing as religious selfishness. Let us count it a sorrowful thing to go to heaven alone, and let us seek to draw companions with us. We ought never to forget that every man, woman, and child around us will soon be either in heaven or hell. Let us say to others as Moses did to Jethro, "Come with us, and we will do thee good." (Num. x. 29.) O it is indeed a true saying, "He that watereth shall be watered himself." (Prov. xi. 25.) The selfish Christian has little idea what he is missing.

But above all, let us learn to live the life of faith in Jesus more than we have hitherto. Ever to be found by the fountain side,—ever to be eating Christ's body by faith, and drinking Christ's blood by faith,—ever to have before our minds Christ dying for our sins,—Christ rising again for our justification,—Christ interceding for us at God's right hand,—Christ soon coming again to gather us to Himself,—this is the mark which we should have continually before our eyes. We may

---

36 "A soul clothed with Christ, stooping to any sinful delight, or an ardent pursuit of anything earthly, though lawful, doth wonderfully degrade itself. Methinks it is as a king's son in his princely apparel playing the scullion, sitting down to turn the spit."—*Archbishop Leighton*. 1670.

fall short, but let us aim high. Let us walk in the full light of the Sun of righteousness, and then our graces will grow. Let us not be like trees on a north wall, weak and unfruitful, and cold. Let us rather strive to be like the sunflower, and to follow the great fountain of light wherever He goes, and to see Him with open face. Oh for an eye more quick to discern His leadings! Oh for an ear more ready to hear his voice![37]

Let us say to everything in the world that interferes between ourselves and Jesus, "stand aside;" and let us dread *allowing* ourselves in the least evil habits, lest insensibly they rise up like a mist and hide Him from our eyes. In His light alone shall we see light and feel warmth, and separate from Him we shall find the world a dark and cold wilderness. We sholud call to mind the request of the Athenian philosopher when the mightiest monarch on earth asked him what he desired most; "I have," said he, "but one request to make, and that is that you would *stand from between me and the sun*." Let this be the spirit in which you and I are found continually. Let us think lightly of the world's gifts. Let us sit calmly under its cares. Let us care for nothing, if we may only ever see the King's face, if we may only ever *abide in Christ*.

And now, Reader, with every kind and Christian wish for your soul's happiness, I commend you to the only wise God, our Saviour. He is able to keep you from

---

37 "Look not for any blessing out of Christ; and in and by and from Him look for all blessings. Let Him be thy life; and wish not to live longer than thou art quickened by Him. Find Him thy wisdom, righteousness, sanctification, redemption; thy riches, thy strength, thy glory." —*Bishop Hall*. 1640.

"All our work now is to be well acquainted with Christ in the way. Christ is both the way and the home. We must be walking in Him and travelling towards Him: and He is our guide and leader in the way. The soul and life of grace, is in living on Him by faith, and the happiness of heaven is in living with Him forever." —*Traill*. 1690.

falling, and to present you faultless before the presence of His glory with exceeding joy.

IV. Are you Holy?

"Holiness, without which no man shall see the Lord."
Hebrews xii. 14.

Reader,—

I offer you this text as a subject for self-inquiry; and I invite you this day to think over the question before your eyes, "*Are you holy?*"

It is a question that can never be out of season. The wise man tells us, "There is a time to weep, and a time to laugh,—a time to keep silence, and a time to speak;" (Eccles. iii. 4, 7.) but there is no time, no, not a day, in which a man ought not to be holy. Reader, are you?

It is a question that concerns all ranks and conditions of men. Some are rich, and some are poor,—some learned, and some unlearned,—some masters, and some servants;—but there is no rank or condition in life in which a man ought not to be holy. Reader, are you?

I ask to be heard to-day about this question. How stands the account between your souls and God? Stay a little, I beseech you, while I reason with you about holiness. I believe I might have chosen a subject more popular and pleasant. I am sure I might have found one more easy to handle. But I feel deeply I could not have chosen one more important and more profitable to your soul. It is a solemn thing to hear God saying, "Without holiness no man can see the Lord." (Heb. xii. 14.)

I shall endeavor, by God's help, to set before you what true holiness is,—the reasons why it is so needful,—and the way in which alone it can be attained. The

Lord grant you may see and feel the importance of the subject, and lay down this paper, when you have read it, a wiser and a better man.

1. First then let me try to show you *what true holiness is,—what sort of persons are those whom God calls holy*.

A man may go great lengths and yet never reach true holiness. It is not knowledge,—Balaam had that: nor great profession,—Judas Iscariot had that: nor doing many things,—Herod had that: nor zeal for certain matters in religion,—Jehu had that: nor morality and outward respectability of conduct,—the young ruler had that: nor taking pleasure in hearing preachers,—the Jews in Ezekiel's time had that: nor keeping company with godly people,—Joab and Gehazi and Demas had that. Yet none of these were holy. These things alone are not holiness. A man may have any one of them, and yet never see the Lord.

What then is true holiness? It is a hard question to answer. I do not mean that I find a want of matter on the subject. But I fear lest I should give a defective view of holiness, and not say all that ought to be said; or lest I should speak things about it that ought not to be spoken, and so do harm. Suffer me, however, to say a few words that may help to clear your mind. Remember only, when I have said all, that my account is but a poor imperfect outline at the best.

Holiness is *the habit of being of one mind with God*, according as we find His mind described in Scripture. It is the habit of agreeing in God's judgment,—hating what He hates,—loving what He loves,—and measuring everything in this world by the standard of His word. He who most entirely agrees with God, he is the most holy man.

A holy man will *endeavor to shun every known sin, and to keep every known commandment*. He will have a decided bent of mind towards God,—a hearty desire to do His will,—a greater fear of displeasing Him than of displeasing the world, and a love to all His ways. He will feel what Paul felt when he said, "I delight in the law of God after the inward man," (Rom. vii. 22,) and what David felt when he said, "I esteem *all* thy precepts concerning all things to be right, and I hate *every* false way." (Psalm cxix. 128.)

A holy man will *strive to be like our Lord Jesus Christ*; to have the mind that was in Him, and to be conformed to His image. It will be his aim to bear with and forgive others, even as Christ forgave us,—to be unselfish, even as Christ pleased not Himself,—to walk in love, even as Christ loved us,—to be lowly-minded and humble, even as Christ made Himself of no reputation and humbled Himself. He will remember that Christ was a faithful witness for the truth,—that He came not to do His own will,—that it was His meat and drink to do His Father's will,—that He would stoop to any work in order to minister to others,—that He was meek and patient under undeserved insults,—that He thought more of godly poor men than of kings,—that He was full of love and compassion to sinners,—that He was bold and uncompromising in denouncing sin,—that He sought not the praise of men, when He might have had it,—that He went about doing good,—that He was separate from worldly people,—that He continued instant in prayer,—that He would not let even His nearest relations stand in His way when God's work was to be done. These things a holy man will try to remember. By them He will endeavor to shape his course in life. He will lay to heart the saying of John, "He that saith he abideth in Christ ought himself also so to walk, even as He walked;" (1 John ii. 6,) and the saying of Peter, that "Christ suffered for us, leaving us an example that ye should follow His steps." (1 Peter ii. 21.) Much time would be saved, and much sin prevented, if men would oftener ask themselves the question, "What would Christ have said and done, if He were in my place?"

But time would fail me if I were to mention all the things which go to make up holiness of character. Still I must ask you to bear with me while I name a few things which come uppermost in my thoughts. The days we live in make me anxious that there should be no mistake upon this subject. How can we know whether we are holy, unless we have a clear view of what holiness takes in?

A holy man will follow after *meekness*, long-suffering, gentleness, kind temper, government of his tongue. He will bear much, forbear much, overlook much, and be slow to talk of standing on his rights. You see a bright example of this in the behavior of David when Shimei cursed him,—and of Moses when Aaron and Miriam spake against him. (2 Sam. xvi. 10. Num. xii. 3.)

A holy man will follow after *temperance and self-denial*. He will labor to mortify the desires of his body,—to crucify his flesh with its affections and lusts,—to curb his passions,—to restrain his carnal inclinations, lest at any time they break loose. Oh! what a word is that of the Lord Jesus to the apostles, "Take heed to yourselves, lest at any time your hearts be overcharged with surfeiting and drunkenness and cares of this life;" (Luke xxi. 34,) and that of the apostle Paul, "I keep under my body and bring it into subjection, lest that by any means when I have preached to others, I myself should be a cast-away." (1 Cor. ix. 27.)

A holy man will follow after *charity and brotherly kindness*. He will endeavor to observe the golden rule, of doing as he would have men do to him, and speaking as he would have men speak to him. He will be full of affection towards his brethren,—their bodies their property, their characters, their feelings, their souls. "He that loveth another," says Paul, "hath fulfilled the law." (Rom. xiii. 8.) He will abhor all lying, slandering, backbiting, cheating, dishonesty, and unfair dealing, even in the least things. The shekel and cubit of the sanctuary were larger than those in common use. Alas! what condemning words are the thirteenth chapter of the first of Corinthians, and the Sermon on the Mount, when laid alongside the conduct of many professing Christians.

A holy man will follow after a spirit of *mercy and benevolence towards others*. He will not stand all the day idle. He will not be content with doing no harm,—he will try to do good. He will strive to be useful in his day and generation, and to lessen the spiritual wants and misery around him, as far as he can. Such was Dorcas, full of good works and almsdeeds, which she did,—not merely purposed and talked about, *but did*. Such an one was Paul, "I will very gladly spend and be spent for you," he says, "though the more abundantly I love you the less I be loved." (1 Cor. xvi. 12, 15.)

A holy man will follow after *purity of heart*. He will dread all filthiness and uncleanness of spirit, and seek to avoid all things that might draw him into it. He knows his own heart is like tinder, and will diligently keep clear of the sparks of temptation. Who shall dare to talk of strength, when David can fall? There is many a hint to be gleaned from the ceremonial law. Under it the man who only touched a bone, or a dead body, or a grave, or a diseased person, became at once unclean in the sight of God. And these things were emblems and figures. Few Christians are ever too watchful and too particular about this point.

A holy man will follow after *the fear of God*. I do not mean the fear of a slave, who only works because he is afraid of punishment, and would be idle if he did not dread discovery. I mean rather the fear of a child, who wishes to live and move as if he was always before his father's face, because he loves him. What a noble example Nehemiah gives us of this! When he became governor at Jerusalem he might have been chargeable to the Jews, and required of them money for his support.

The former governors had done so. There was none to blame him if he did. But he says, "So did not I, because of the fear of God." (Nehem. v. 15.)

A holy man will follow after *humility*. He will desire in lowliness of mind to esteem all others better than himself. He will see more evil in his own heart than in any other in the world. He will understand something of Abraham's feeling, when he says, "I am dust and ashes," and Jacob's, when he says, "I am less than the least of all thy mercies," and Job's, when he says, "I am vile," and Paul's, when he says, "I am chief of sinners." Holy Bradford, that faithful martyr of Christ, would sometimes finish his letters with these words, "A most miserable sinner, John Bradford." Good old Mr. Grimshaw's last words, when he lay on his death-bed, were these, "Here goes an unprofitable servant."

A holy man will follow after *faithfulness in all the duties and relations of life*. He will try, not merely to fill his place as well as others, but even better, because he has higher motives and more help than they. Those words of Paul should never be forgotten, "Whatever ye do, do it heartily as unto the Lord." — "Not slothful in business, fervent in spirit, serving the Lord." (Colos. iii. 23. Rom. xii. 11.) Holy persons should aim at doing everything well, and should be ashamed of allowing themselves to do anything ill, if they can help it. Like Daniel, they should seek to give no occasion against themselves, except as concerning the law of their God. They should strive to be good husbands, and good wives; good parents and good children; good masters and good servants; good neighbors, good friends, good men of business, and good subjects. Holiness is worth little indeed, if it does not bear this kind of fruit. The Lord Jesus puts a searching question to His people, when he says, "What do ye more than others?" (Matt. v. 47.)

Last, but not least, a holy man will follow after *spiritual mindedness*. He will endeavor to set his affections entirely on things above, and to hold things on earth with a very loose hand. He will not neglect the business of the life that now is, but the first place in his mind and thoughts will be given to the life to come. He will aim to live like one whose treasure is in heaven, and to pass through this world like a stranger and pilgrim travelling to his home. To commune with God in prayer, in the Bible, and in the assembly of His people,—these things will be the holy man's chiefest enjoyments. He will value every thing, and place, and company, just in proportion as it draws him nearer to God. He will enter into something of David's feeling, when he says, "My soul followeth after thee." "Thou art my portion." (Psalm lxiii. 8.; cxix. 57.)

Such is the outline of holiness, which I set before you; such is the character which those who are called holy follow after.

But here let me say, I trust no man will misunderstand me. I am not without fear that my meaning will be mistaken, and the description I have given of holiness will discourage some tender conscience. I would not willingly make one righteous heart sad, or throw a stumbling-block in any believer's way.

I do not tell you for a moment that holiness shuts out the presence of *indwelling sin*. No! far from it. It is the greatest misery of a holy man that he carries about with him a body of death,—that often when he would do good evil is present with him,—that the old man is clogging all his movements, and as it were, trying to draw him back at every step he takes. But it is the excellence of a holy man that he is not at peace with indwelling sin, as others are. He hates it, mourns over it, and longs to be free from its company. The work of sanctification within him is like the wall of Jerusalem, the building goes forward, "even in troublous times." (Dan. ix. 25.)

Neither do I tell you that holiness comes to ripeness and perfection all at once, or that these graces I have touched on must be found in full bloom and vigor before you can call a man holy. No! far from it. Sanctification is always a *progressive work*. Some men's graces are in the blade, some in the ear, and some are like full corn in the ear. All must have a beginning. We must never despise the day of small things. And sanctification in the very best is an *imperfect work*. The history of the brightest saints that ever lived will contain many a "but" and "howbeit," and "notwithstanding," before you reach the end. The gold will never be without some dross,—the light will never shine without some clouds, until we reach the heavenly Jerusalem. The sun himself has spots upon his face. The holiest men have many a blemish and defect when weighed in the balance of the sanctuary. Their life is a continued warfare with sin, the world, and the devil; and sometimes you will see them not overcoming, but overcome. The flesh is ever lusting against the spirit, and the spirit against the flesh, and in many things they offend all.

But still, for all this, I am sure that to have such a character as I have faintly drawn, is the heart's desire and prayer of all true Christians. They press towards it, if they do not reach it. They may not attain to it, but they always aim at it. It is what they fain would be, if it is not what they are.

And this I do mean to say, that true holiness is a great reality. It is something in a man that can be seen, and known, and marked, and felt, by all around him. It is light: if it exists it will show itself. It is salt: if it exists its savor will be perceived. It is a precious ointment: if it exists its presence cannot be hid.

I am sure the little I know of my own heart makes me ready to make allowance for much backsliding, for much occasional deadness. I know a road may lead from one point to another, and yet have many a winding and turn; and a man may be truly holy, and yet be drawn aside by many an infirmity. Gold is not the less gold because mingled with alloy, nor light the less light because faint and dim, nor grace the less grace because young and weak. But, after every allowance, I cannot see how any man deserves to be called holy, who wilfully allows himself in sins, and is not humbled and ashamed because of them. I dare not call any one holy who makes a habit of wilfully neglecting known duties, and wilfully doing what he knows God has commanded him not to do. Well, says Owen, "I do not understand how a man can be a true believer unto whom sin is not the greatest burden, sorrow, and trouble."

Reader, such is holiness. Examine yourself whether you are acquainted with it. Prove your own self.

II. Let me try, in the next place, *to show you some reasons why holiness is so important*.

Can holiness save us? Can holiness put away sin,—cover iniquities,—make satisfaction for transgressions,—pay our debt to God? No! not a whit. God forbid that I should ever tell you so. Holiness can do none of these things. The brightest saints are all unprofitable servants. Our purest works are no better than filthy rags, when tried by the light of God's holy law. The white robe which Jesus offers, and faith puts on, must be our only righteousness,—the name of Christ our only confidence,—the Lamb's book of life our only title to heaven. With all our holiness we are no better than sinners. Our best things are stained and tainted with imperfection. They are all more or less incomplete,— wrong in the motive, or defective in the performance. By the deeds of the law shall no child of Adam ever be justified. "By grace are ye saved through faith, and that not of yourselves, it is the gift of God: not of works, lest any man should boast." (Ephes. ii. 8, 9.)

Why then is holiness so important? Why does the apostle say, "without it no man shall see the Lord?" Let me set before you a few reasons.

For one thing we must be holy, because *the voice of God in Scripture plainly commands it*. The Lord Jesus says to His people, "Except your righteousness shall exceed the righteousness of the Scribes and Pharisees, ye shall in no case enter into the kingdom of heaven." (Matt. v. 20.) "Be ye perfect, even as your Father which is in heaven is perfect." (Matt. v. 48.) Paul tells the Thessalonians, "This is the will of God, even your sanctification." (1 Thess. iv. 3.) And Peter says, "As He which hath called you is holy, so be ye holy in all manner of conversation. Because it is written, Be ye holy for I am holy." (1 Peter i. 15, 16.) "In this," says Leighton, "law and Gospel agree."

We must be holy, because this is one grand *end and purpose for which Christ came into the world*. Paul writes to the Corinthians, "He died for all, that they which live should not henceforth live unto themselves, but unto Him which died for them and rose again." (2 Cor. v. 15.) And to the Ephesians, "Christ loved the Church and gave Himself for it, that He might sanctify and cleanse it." (Ephes. v. 25, 26.) And to Titus, "He gave Himself for us, that He might redeem us from all iniquity, and purify unto Himself a peculiar people, zealous of good works." (Titus ii. 14.) In short, to talk of men being saved from the *guilt* of sin, without being at the same time saved from its *power* in their hearts, is to contradict the witness of all Scripture. Are believers said to be elect?—it is "through sanctification of the Spirit." Are they predestinated?—it is "to be conformed to the image of God's Son." Are they chosen?—it is "that they may be holy." Are they called?—it is "with a holy calling." Are they afflicted?—it is that they may be "partakers of holiness." Jesus is a complete Saviour. He does not merely take away the guilt of a believer's sin, He does more,—He breaks its power.

We must be holy, because this is the *only sound evidence that we have a saving faith in our Lord Jesus Christ*. The twelfth Article of our Church says truly, "Although good works cannot put away our sins, and endure the severity of God's judgment; yet are they pleasing and acceptable to God in Christ, and do spring out necessarily of a true and lively faith; insomuch that by them a lively faith may be as evidently known as a tree discerned by its fruits." James warns us there is such a thing as a dead faith,—a faith which goes no further than the profession of the lips, and has no influence on a man's character. (Jam. ii. 17.) True saving faith is a very different kind of thing. True faith will always show itself by its fruits, it will sanctify,—it will work by love,—it will overcome the world,—it will purify the heart. I know that people are fond of talking about "death-bed evidences." They will rest on words spoken in the hours of fear and pain and weakness, as if they might take comfort in them about the friends they lose. But I am afraid in ninety-nine cases out of a hundred such evidences are not to be depended on. I suspect men generally die just as they have lived. The only safe evidence that you are one with Christ, and Christ in you, is *a holy life*. They that live unto the Lord are generally the only people who die in the Lord. If we would die the death of the righteous, let us not rest in slothful desires only, let us seek to live his life. It is a true saying of Traill's, "that man's state is naught, and his faith unsound, that finds not his hopes of glory purifying to his heart and life."

We must be holy, because this is the *only proof that we love the Lord Jesus Christ in sincerity*. This is a point on which He has spoken Himself most plainly in the fourteenth and fifteenth chapters of John. "If ye love me, keep my commandments." "He that hath my commandments, and keepeth them, he it is that loveth me."

"If a man love me he will keep my saying." "Ye are my friends if ye do whatsoever I command you." Plainer words than these it would be difficult to find, and woe to those who neglect them! Surely that man must be in an unhealthy state of soul who can think of all that Jesus suffered, and yet cling to those sins for which that suffering was undergone. It was sin that wove the crown of thorns,—it was sin that pierced our Lord's hands, and feet, and side,—it was sin that brought Him to Gethsemane and Calvary, to the cross, and to the grave. Cold must our hearts be, if we do not hate sin, and labor to get rid of it, though we have to cut off the right hand, and pluck out the right eye in doing it.

We must be holy, because this is the *only sound evidence that we are true children of God*. Children in this world are generally like their parents. Some, doubtless, are more so, and some less,—but it is seldom indeed that you cannot trace a kind of family likeness. And it is much the same with the children of God. If men have no likeness to the Father in heaven, it is vain to talk of their being His sons. If we know nothing of holiness we may flatter ourselves as we please, but we have not the Holy Spirit dwelling in us,—we are dead, and must be brought to life again,—we are lost, and must be found. As many as are led by the Spirit of God, they, and they only, are the sons of God. (Rom. viii. 14.) We must show by our lives the family we belong to,—we must let men see by our good conversation that we are indeed the children of the Holy One, or our son-ship is but an empty name. "Say not," says Gurnall, "that thou hast royal blood in thy veins, and art born of God, except thou canst prove thy pedigree by daring to be holy."

We must be holy, because this is the *most likely way to do good to others*. We cannot live to ourselves only in this world. Our lives will always be doing either good or harm to those who see them. They are a silent sermon which all can read. It is sad indeed when they are a sermon for the devil's cause, and not for God's. I believe that far more is done for Christ's kingdom by the holy living of believers, than we are at all aware. There is a reality about such living which makes men feel, and obliges them to think. It carries a weight and influence with it which nothing else can give. It makes religion beautiful, and draws men to consider it like a lighthouse seen afar off. The day of judgment will prove that many besides husbands have been won *"without the word,"* by a holy life. (1 Peter iii. 1.) You may talk to people about the doctrines of the Gospel, and few will listen, and still fewer understand. But your life is an argument that none can escape. There is a meaning about holiness which not even the most unlearned can help taking in. They may not understand justification, but they can understand charity.

And I believe there is far more harm done by unholy and inconsistent Christians than we are at all aware. Such men are among Satan's best allies. They pull down by their lives what ministers build with their lips. They cause the chariot wheels of the Gospel to drive heavily. They supply the children of this world with a never-ending excuse for remaining as they are. "I cannot see the use of so much religion," said an irreligious tradesmen not long ago; "I observe that some of my customers are always talking about the Gospel, and faith, and election, and the blessed promises and so forth;—and yet these very people think nothing of cheating me of pence and half-pence, when they have an opportunity. Now if religious persons can do such things, I do not see what good there is in religion." Oh! Reader, I blush to be obliged to read such things. I fear that Christ's name is too often blasphemed because of the lives of Christians. Let us take heed lest the blood of souls be required at our hands. From murder of souls by inconsistency and loose walking, good Lord deliver us! Oh! for the sake of others, if for no other reason, let us strive to be holy!

We must be holy, *because our present comfort depends much upon it*. We cannot be too often reminded of this. We are sadly apt to forget that there is a close connection between sin and sorrow, holiness and happiness, sanctification and consolation. God has so wisely ordered it, that our well-being and our well-doing are linked together. He has mercifully provided that even in this world it shall be man's *interest* to be holy. Our justification is not by works,—our calling and election are not according to our works,—but it is vain for any one to suppose that he will have a lively *sense* of his justification, or an *assurance* of his calling, so long as he does not strive to live a holy life. A believer may as soon expect to feel the sun's rays upon a dark and cloudy day, as to feel strong consolation in Christ, while he does not follow Him fully. When the disciples forsook the Lord and fled, they escaped danger, but they were miserable and sad. When shortly after they confessed Him boldly before men, they were cast into prison and beaten, but we are told, "They rejoiced that they were counted worthy to suffer shame for His name." (Acts v. 41.) Oh! for our own sakes, if there were no other reason, let us strive to be holy! He that follows Jesus most fully, will always follow Him most comfortably.

Lastly, we must be holy, *because without holiness on earth we should never be prepared to enjoy heaven*. Heaven is a holy place. The Lord of heaven is a holy Being. The angels are holy creatures. Holiness is written on everything in heaven. The book of Revelation says expressly, "there shall in nowise enter into it, anything that defileth, neither whatsoever worketh abomination, or maketh a lie." (Rev. xxi. 27.)

Reader, how shall we ever find a place in heaven, if we die unholy! Death works no change. The grave makes no alteration. Each will rise again with the same

IV. Are you Holy?

character in which he breathed his last. Where will our place be if we are strangers to holiness now?

Suppose for a moment that you were allowed to enter heaven without holiness. What would you do? What possible enjoyment could you feel there? To which of all the saints would you join yourself, and by whose side would you sit down? Their pleasures are not your pleasures, their tastes are not your tastes, their character not your character. How could you possibly be happy if you had not been holy on earth?

Now perhaps, you love the company of the light and the careless, the worldly-minded and the covetous, the reveller and the pleasure-seeker, the ungodly and the profane. There will be none such in heaven.

Now perhaps, you think the saints of God too strict, and particular, and serious. You rather avoid them. You have no delight in their society. There will be no other company in heaven.

Now perhaps, you think praying, and Scripture reading, and hymn-singing, dull and melancholy, and stupid work, a thing to be tolerated now and then, but not enjoyed. You reckon the Sabbath a burden, and a weariness; you could not possibly spend more than a small part of it in worshipping God. But remember, heaven is a never-ending Sabbath. The inhabitants thereof rest not day or night, saying, "Holy, holy, holy, Lord God Almighty," and singing the praise of the Lamb. How could an unholy man find pleasure in occupation such as this?

Think you that such an one would delight to meet David, and Paul, and John, after a life spent in doing the very things they spoke against? Would he take sweet counsel with them, and find that he and they had much in common? Think you, above all, that he would rejoice to meet Jesus, the Crucified One, face to face, after cleaving to the sins for which He died,—after loving His enemies, and despising his friends? Would he stand before him in confidence, and join in the cry, "This is our God, we have waited for Him, we will be glad, and rejoice in his salvation?" Think you not rather that the tongue of an unholy man would cleave to the roof of his mouth with shame, and his only desire would be to be cast out? He would feel a stranger in a land he knew not, a black sheep amidst Christ's holy flock. The voice of Cherubim and Seraphim, the song of Angels and Archangels, and all the company of heaven would be a language he could not understand. The very air would seem an air he could not breathe.

Reader, I know not what you may think, but to me it does seem clear, that heaven would be a miserable place to an unholy man. It cannot be otherwise. People may say, in a vague way, "they hope to go to heaven," but they do not consider what they say. There must be a certain *meetness* for the inheritance of the saints in light. Our hearts must be somewhat in tune. To reach the holiday of glory we must pass through the training school of grace. Reader, you must be heavenly minded, and have heavenly tastes, in the life that now is, or else you will never find yourself in heaven in the life to come.

And now let me wind up all with a few words, by way of application.

1. For one thing, let me ask every one who may read these pages, *Are you holy?* Listen, I pray you, to the question I put to you this day. Do you know anything of the holiness of which I have been speaking?

I do not ask whether you keep to your church regularly,—whether you have been baptized, and receive the Lord's Supper,—whether you have the name of Christian;—I ask something more than all this, *Are you holy, or are you not?*

I do not ask whether you approve of holiness in others,—whether you like to read the lives of holy people, and to talk of holy things, and to have on your table holy books,—whether you mean to be holy, and hope you will be holy some day,—I ask something further, *Are you yourself holy this very day, or are you not?*

And why do I ask so straitly, and press the question so strongly? I do it because the text says, "Without holiness no man shall see the Lord." It is written, it is not my fancy—it is the Bible, not my private opinion,—it is the word of God, not of man, *"Without holiness no man shall see the Lord."*

Oh! Reader, what words are these! What thoughts come across my mind, as I write them down! I look at the world, and see the greater part of it lying in wickedness. I look at professing Christians, and see the vast majority having nothing of Christianity but the name. I turn to the Bible, and I hear the Spirit saying, "Without holiness no man shall see the Lord."

Surely it is a text that ought to make you consider your ways, and search your hearts. Surely it should raise within you solemn thoughts, and send you to prayer.

You may try and put me off, by saying, "you feel much, and think much, about these things, far more than many suppose." I answer, This is not the point. The poor lost souls in hell do as much as this. The great question is, not what you *think*, and what you *feel*, but what you DO.

You may say, "it was never meant that all Christians should be holy, and that holiness, such as I have described, is only for great saints, and people of uncommon gifts." I answer, I cannot see that in Scripture. I read that *"every man* who has hope in Christ, purifieth himself." (1 John iii. 3.)—"Without holiness *no man* shall see the Lord."

You may say, "it is impossible to be so holy, and to do our duty in this life at the same time: the thing cannot be done." I answer, You are mistaken. It *can* be done. With God on your side nothing is impossible. It *has* been done by many. David, and Obadiah, and Daniel, and the servants of Nero's household, are all examples that go to prove it.

You may say, "if you were so holy, you would be unlike other people." I answer, I know it well. It is just what I want you to be. Christ's true servants always were unlike the world around them, a separate nation, a peculiar people, and you must be so too, if you would be saved.

You may say, "at this rate very few will be saved." I answer, I know it. Jesus said so 1800 years ago. Few will be saved, because few will take the trouble to seek salvation. Men will not deny themselves the pleasure of sin, and their own way for a season. For this they turn their backs on an inheritance incorruptible, undefiled, and that fadeth not away. "Ye will not come unto me," says Jesus, "that ye might have life." (John v. 40.)

You may say, "These are hard sayings, the way is very narrow." I answer, I know it. Jesus said so 1800 years ago. He always said that men must take up the cross daily, that they must be ready to cut off hand or foot, if they would be His disciples. It is in religion as it is in other things, "there are no gains without pains." That which costs nothing is worth nothing.

Reader, whatever you may think or say, you must be holy, if you would see the Lord. Where is your Christianity, if you are not? Show it to me without holiness, if you can. You must not merely have a Christian name, and Christian knowledge, you must have a Christian *character* also. You must be a saint on earth, if ever you mean to be a saint in heaven. God has said it, and He will not go back,—"Without holiness no man shall see the Lord." "The Pope's calendar," says Jenkyn, "only makes saints of the *dead*, but Scripture requires sanctity in the *living*." "Let not men deceive themselves," says Owen, "sanctification is a qualification indispensably necessary unto those who will be under the conduct of the Lord Christ unto salvation: He leads none to heaven, but whom He sanctifies on the earth. This living Head will not admit of dead members."

Surely you will not wonder that Scripture says, "Ye must be born again." (John iii. 7.) Surely it is clear as noon-day that many a man needs a complete change,—a new heart,—a new nature,—if ever he is to be saved. Old things must pass away,—he must become a new creature. Without holiness no man, be he who he may, no man shall see the Lord.

2. Let me, for another thing, speak a little to every believer who reads these pages. I ask you this question, *"Do you think you feel the importance of holiness as much as you should?"*

I own I fear the temper of the times about this subject. I doubt exceedingly whether it holds that place which it deserves in the thoughts and attention of some of the Lord's people. I would humbly suggest that we are apt to overlook the doctrine of *growth in grace*, and that we do not sufficiently consider how very far a person may go in a profession of religion, and yet have no grace, and be dead in God's sight after all. I believe that Judas Iscariot seemed very like the other apostles. When the Lord warned them one would betray Him, no one said, "Is it Judas?" We had better think more about Sardis and Laodicea than we do.

I have no desire to make an idol of holiness. I do not wish to dethrone Christ, and put holiness in His place. But I must candidly say, I wish sanctification was more thought of in this day than it seems to be, and I therefore take occasion to press the subject on all believers into whose hands this paper may fall.

I fear it is sometimes forgotten, that God has married together justification and sanctification. They are distinct and different things beyond question, but one is never found without the other. All justified people are sanctified, and all sanctified are justified. What God has joined together let no man dare put asunder. Tell me not of your justification, unless you have also some marks of sanctification. Boast not of Christ's work *for you*, unless you can show us the Spirit's work *in you*. Think not that Christ and the Spirit can ever be divided.

Reader, if you are a believer, I doubt not you know these things, but I think it good to put you in remembrance of them. Prove that you know them by your life. Try to keep in view this text more continually, "Follow holiness, without which no man shall see the Lord."

I must frankly say, I wish there was not such an excessive *sensitiveness* on the subject of holiness as I sometimes perceive in the minds of believers. A man might really think it was a dangerous subject to handle, so cautiously is it touched. Yet surely when we have exalted Christ as the way, the truth, and the life, we cannot err in speaking strongly about what should be the character of His people. Well says Rutherford, "The way that crieth down duties and sanctification, is not the way of grace. Believing and doing are blood friends."

There is a thing I would say with reverence,—but say it I must,—I sometimes fear if Christ were on earth now, there are not a few who would think His preaching legal; and if Paul were writing his Epistles, there are those who would think he had better not write the latter part of most of them as he did. But let us remember that the Lord Jesus *did* speak the Sermon on the Mount, and that the Epistle to the Ephesians contains six chapters, and not four. I grieve to feel obliged to speak in this way, but I am sure there is a cause.

The great divine, Owen, said some two hundred years ago, that there were people whose whole religion seemed to consist in going about complaining of their own corruptions, and telling every one they could do nothing of themselves.

Reader, I put it to yourself,—might not the same thing be said with truth of some of Christ's professing people in this day?

I know there are texts in Scripture that warrant such complaints. I do not object to them when they come from men who walk in the steps of the apostle Paul, and fight a good fight, as he did, against sin, the devil, and the world. But I never like such complaints when I see grounds for suspecting, as I often do, that they are only a cloak to cover spiritual laziness, and an excuse for spiritual sloth. If we say with Paul, "O wretched man that I am," let us also be able to say with him, "I press toward the mark." Let us not quote his example in one thing, while we do not follow him in another. (Rom. vii. 24. Phil. iii. 14.)

I do not set up myself to be better than other people, and if any one asks, "What are you, that you talk in this way?" I answer, "I am a very poor creature indeed." But I tell you I cannot read the Bible without desiring to see many believers more spiritual, more holy, more single-eyed, more heavenly-minded, more whole-hearted than they are. I want to see among us more of a pilgrim spirit, a more decided separation from the world, a conversation more evidently in heaven, a closer walk with God,—and therefore I have spoken as I have.

Is it not true that we need a higher standard of personal holiness in this day? Where is our patience? Where is our zeal? Where is our love? Where are our works? Where is the power of religion to be seen, as it was in times gone by? Where is that unmistakable tone that used to distinguish the saints of old, and shake the world? Verily our silver has become dross, our wine mixed with water. We are all more than half asleep. The night is far spent, and the day is at hand. Let us awake and sleep no more. Let us open our eyes more widely than we have done hitherto. Let us lay aside every weight, and the sin that doth so easily beset us. Let us cleanse ourselves from all filthiness of flesh and spirit, and perfect holiness in the fear of God. "Did Christ die," says Owen, "and shall sin live? Was He crucified in the world, and shall our affections to the world be quick and lively? Oh! where is the spirit of Him, who by the cross of Christ was crucified to the world, and the world to him?"

3. Let me, in the last place, offer a *word of advice to all who desire to be holy*.

Would you be holy? Would you become new creatures? *Then begin with Christ*. You will do just nothing till you feel your sin and weakness, and flee to Him. He is the beginning of all holiness. He is not wisdom and righteousness only to His people, but sanctification also. Men sometimes try to make themselves holy *first of all*, and sad work they make of it. They toil and labor, and turn over many new leaves, and make many changes, and yet, like the woman with the issue of blood before she came to Christ, they feel nothing bettered, but rather worse. They run in vain, and labor in vain, and little wonder, for they are beginning at the wrong end. They are building up a wall of sand; their work runs down as fast as they throw it up. They are baling water out of a leaky vessel; the leak gains on them, not they on the leak. Other foundation of holiness can no man lay than that which Paul laid, even Christ Jesus. Without Christ we can do nothing. It is a strong but true saying of Traill's, "Wisdom out of Christ is damning folly;—righteousness out of Christ is guilt and condemnation;—sanctification out of Christ is filth and sin;—redemption out of Christ is bondage and slavery."

Would you be holy? Would you be partakers of the divine nature? Then *go to Christ*. Wait for nothing. Wait for nobody. Linger not. Think not to make yourself ready. Go and say to Him, in the words of that beautiful hymn,—

> "*Nothing in my hand I bring,*
> *Simply to thy cross I cling;*
> *Naked, flee to thee for dress;*
> *Helpless, look to thee for grace.*"

There is not a brick nor a stone laid in the work of our sanctification, till we go to Christ. Holiness is His special gift to His believing people. Holiness is the work He carries on in their hearts by the Spirit whom He puts within them. He is anointed a Prince and a Saviour, to give repentance as well as remission of sins. To as many as receive Him He gives power to become sons of God. (John i. 12.)

Holiness comes not of blood,—parents cannot give it to their children: nor yet of the will of the flesh,—man cannot produce it in himself: nor yet of the will of man, ministers cannot give it you by baptism. Holiness comes from Christ. It is the result of vital union with Him. It is the fruit of being a living branch of the true vine. Go then to Christ, and say, "Lord, not only save me from the guilt of sin, but send the Spirit, whom thou didst promise, and save me from its power. Make me holy. Teach me to do thy will."

Would you continue holy? Then *abide in Christ*. He says Himself, "Abide in me and I in you,—he that abideth in me and I in him, the same beareth much fruit." (John xv. 4, 5) It pleased the Father that in Him should all fulness dwell,—a full supply for all a believer's wants. He is the Physician to whom you must daily go, if you would keep well. He is the manna which you must daily eat, and the rock of which you must daily drink. His arm is the arm on which you must daily lean, as you come up out of the wilderness of this world. You must not only be rooted, you must also be *built up* in Him. Paul was a man of God indeed,—a holy man,—a growing, thriving Christian,—and what was the secret of it all? He was one to whom Christ was "all in all." He was ever "looking unto Jesus." "I can do all things," he says, "through Christ which strengthened me." "I live, yet not I, but Christ liveth in me. The life that I now live, I live by the faith of the Son of God." (Phil. iv. 13. Gal. ii. 20.) Reader, go and do likewise.

Now may you and I know these things by experience, and not by hearsay only. May we all feel the importance of holiness far more than we have ever done yet. May our years be *holy years* with our souls, and then I know they will be happy ones. Whether we live, may we live unto the Lord; or whether we die, may we die unto the Lord: or if He come for us, may we be found in peace, without spot, and blameless.

And now, if I have erred in anything that I have written, may the good Lord pardon me, and show me what is the mind of the Spirit. But if, as I believe, I have told you the truth, may the Lord open your heart, and make it a word in season to you, and all who read it.

V. ONLY ONE WAY

"Neither is there salvation in any other; for there is none other name under heaven, given among men, whereby we must be saved."

ACTS IV. 12.

READER,—

These words are striking in themselves. But they are much more striking, if you consider when, and by whom they were spoken.

They were spoken by a poor and friendless Christian, in the midst of a persecuting Jewish Council. It was a grand confession of Christ.

They were spoken by the lips of the Apostle Peter. This is the man who a few weeks before forsook Jesus and fled. This is the very man who three times over denied his Lord. There is another spirit in him now. He stands up boldly before Priests and Sadducees, and tells them the truth to their face: "This is the stone that was set at naught of you builders, which is become the head of the corner. Neither is there salvation in any other: for there is none other name under heaven, given among men, whereby we must be saved."

Now, I need hardly tell you, this text is one of the principal foundations on which the Eighteenth Article of the Church of England is built.

That Article runs as follows: "They also are to be had accursed that presume to say that every man shall be saved by the law or sect he professeth, so that he be diligent to frame his life according to that law and the light of nature. For Holy Scripture doth set out unto us only the name of Jesus Christ, whereby men must be saved."

There are few stronger assertions than this throughout the whole thirty-nine Articles. It is the only anathema pronounced by our Church from one end of her confession of faith to the other. The Council of Trent in her decrees anathematizes continually. The Church of England does it once, and once only. And that she does it on good grounds, I propose to show you by an examination of the Apostle Peter's words.

In considering this solemn subject, there are three things I wish to do.

I. First, to show you the doctrine here laid down by the Apostle.

II. Secondly, to show you some reasons why this doctrine must be true.

III. Thirdly, to show you some consequences which naturally flow from the doctrine.

I. *First let me show you the doctrine of the text.*

Let us make sure that we rightly understand what the Apostle Peter means. He says of Christ, "Neither is there salvation in any other: for there is none other name under heaven, given among men, whereby we must be saved." Now what is this? On our clearly seeing this very much depends.

He means that no one can be saved from sin,—its guilt, power, and consequences,—excepting by Jesus Christ.

He means that no one can have peace with God the Father,—obtain pardon in this world,—and escape wrath to come in the next,—excepting through the atonement and mediation of Jesus Christ.

In Christ alone God's rich provision of salvation for sinners is treasured up. By Christ alone God's abundant mercies come down from heaven to earth. Christ's blood alone can cleanse us. Christ's righteousness alone can clothe us. Christ's merit alone can give us a title to heaven. Jews and Gentiles,—learned and unlearned,—kings and poor men,—all alike must either be saved by Jesus, or lost forever.

And the Apostle adds emphatically, "there is none other name under heaven, given among men, whereby we must be saved." There is no other person commissioned, sealed, and appointed by God the Father, to be the Saviour of Sinners, excepting Christ. The keys of life and death are committed to his hand, and all who would be saved must go to Him.

There was but one place of safety in the day when the flood came upon the earth, and that was Noah's ark. All other places and devices,—mountains, towers, trees, rafts, boats,—all were alike useless. So also there is but one hiding-place for the sinner who would escape the storm of God's anger,—he must venture his soul on Christ.

There was but one man to whom the Egyptians could go in the time of famine, when they wanted food. They must go to Joseph. It was a waste of time to go to any one else. So also there is but one to whom hungering souls must go, if they would not perish forever,—they must go to Christ.

There was but one word that could save the lives of the Ephraimites in the day when the Gileadites contended with them, and took the fords of Jordan. (Judges 11) They must say "Shibboleth" or die. Just so there is but one name that will avail us when we stand at the gate of heaven. We must name the name of Jesus as our only hope, or be cast away everlastingly.

Such is the doctrine of the text, "No salvation but by Jesus Christ;—in Him plenty of salvation,—salvation to the uttermost,—salvation for the very chief of sinners;—out of Him no salvation at all." It is in perfect harmony with our Lord's own word in St. John: "I am the way, the truth, and the life; no man cometh unto the Father but by me." (John xiv. 6.) It is the same thing that Paul tells the Corinthians: "Other foundation can no man lay than that is laid, which is Jesus Christ." (1 Cor. iii. 11.) And the same that John tells us in his first Epistle: "God hath given to us eternal life, and this life is in His Son. He that hath the Son hath life, and he that hath not the Son of God hath not life." (1 John v. 12.) All these texts come to one and the same point, — no salvation but by Jesus Christ.

Reader, make sure that you understand this before you pass on. Perhaps you think, this is all old news. Perhaps you feel, "these are ancient things: who knoweth not such truths as these? Of course we believe there is no salvation but by Christ." But mark well what I say; make sure that you understand this doctrine, or else by-and-by you will stumble and be offended at what I have yet to say.

Remember that you are to venture the whole salvation of your soul on Christ, and on Christ only. You are to cast loose completely and entirely from all other hopes and trusts. You are not to rest partly on Christ, — partly on doing all you can, — partly on keeping your Church, — partly on receiving the sacrament. In the matter of your justification Christ is to be *all*. This is the doctrine of the text.

Remember that heaven is before you, and Christ the only door into it; — hell beneath you, and Christ alone able to deliver you from it; — the devil behind you, and Christ the only refuge from his wrath and accusations; — the law against you, and Christ alone able to redeem you; — sin weighing you down, and Christ alone able to put it away. This is the doctrine of the text.

Now do you see it? I hope you do. But I fear many think so, who may find before laying down this paper they do not.

II. *Let me show you, in the second place, some reasons why the doctrine of the text must be true.*

I might cut short this part of the subject by one simple argument, "God says so." "One plain text," said an old divine, "is as good as a thousand reasons."

But I will not do this. I wish to meet the objections that are ready to rise in many hearts against this doctrine, by pointing out the strong foundations on which it stands.

1. Let me then say, for one thing, the doctrine of the text must be true, *because man is what man is.*

Now, what is man? There is one broad sweeping answer, which takes in the whole human race,—man is a sinful being. All children of Adam born into the world, whatever be their name or nation, are corrupt, wicked, and defiled, in the sight of God. Their thoughts, words, ways, and actions, are all more or less defective and imperfect.

Is there no country on the face of the globe where sin does not reign? Is there no happy valley,—no secluded island, where innocence is to be found? Is there no tribe on earth, where far away from civilization, and commerce, and money, and gunpowder, and luxury, and books, morality and purity flourish?—No! Reader, there is none. Look over all the voyages and travels you can lay your hand on, from Columbus down to Cook, and you will see the truth of what I am asserting. The most solitary islands of the Pacific Ocean,—islands cut off from all the rest of the world,—islands where people were alike ignorant of Rome and Paris, London and Jerusalem,—these islands have been found full of impurity, cruelty, and idolatry. The footprints of the devil have been traced on every shore. The veracity of the third of Genesis has everywhere been established. Whatever else savages have been found ignorant of, they have never been found ignorant of sin.

But are there no men and women in the world who are free from this corruption of nature? Have there not been high and exalted souls, who have every now and then lived faultless lives? Have there not been some, if it be only a few, who have done all that God required, and thus proved that sinless perfection is a possibility? — No, Reader, there have been none. Look over all the biographies and lives of the holiest Christians. Mark how the brightest and best of Christ's people have always had the deepest sense of their own defectiveness and corruption. They groan, they mourn, they sigh, they weep over their own short-comings. It is one of the common grounds on which they meet. Patriarchs and Apostles, Fathers and Reformers, Episcopalians and Presbyterians, Luther and Calvin, Knox and Bradford, Rutherford and Bishop Hall, Wesley and Whitefield, Martyn and M'Cheyne, — all are alike agreed in feeling their own sinfulness. The more light they have, the more humble and self-abased they seem to be. The more holy they are, the more they seem to feel their own unworthiness, and to glory, not in themselves, but in Christ.

Now, what does all this tend to prove? To my eyes it seems to prove, that human nature is so tainted and corrupt that, left to himself, no man could be saved. Man's case appears to me a hopeless one without a Saviour, — and that a mighty Saviour too. There must be a Mediator, an Atonement, an Advocate, to make such poor sinful beings acceptable with God: — and I find this nowhere excepting in Jesus Christ. Heaven for man without a mighty Redeemer, — peace with God for man without a mighty Intercessor, — eternal life for man without an eternal Saviour, — in one word, salvation without Christ — all alike appear to me utter impossibilities.

I lay these things before you, and ask you to consider them. I know it is one of the hardest things in the world to realize the sinfulness of sin. *To say* we are all sinners is one thing; to have an idea what sin must be in the sight of God is quite another. Sin is too much part of ourselves, to allow us to see it as it is. We do not *feel* our own moral deformity. We are like those animals in creation which are vile and loathsome to our senses, but are not so to themselves, nor yet to one another. Their loathsomeness is their nature, and they do not perceive it. Our corruption is part and parcel of ourselves, and at our best we have but a feeble comprehension of its intensity.

But this you may be sure of, if you could see your own lives with the eyes of the angels who never fell, you would never doubt this point for a moment. Depend on it, no one can really know what man is, and not see that the doctrine of our text must be true. There can be no salvation except by Christ.

2. Let me say another thing. The doctrine of our text must be true, *because God is what God is*.

Now, what is God? That is a deep question indeed. We know something of his attributes. He has not left himself without witness in creation. He has mercifully revealed to us many things about Himself in His word. We know that God is a Spirit,—eternal,—invisible,—almighty,—the Maker of all things,—the Preserver of all things,—holy,—just,—all-seeing,—all-knowing,—all-remembering,—infinite in mercy, in wisdom, in purity.

But alas! after all, how low and grovelling are our highest ideas, when we come to put down on paper what we believe God to be! How many words and expressions we use whose full meaning we cannot fathom! How many things our tongues say of Him, which our minds are utterly unable to conceive!

How small a part of Him do we see! How little of Him can we possibly know! How mean and paltry are any words of ours to convey any idea of Him who made this mighty world out of nothing, and with whom one day is as a thousand years, and a thousand years as one day! How weak and inadequate are our poor feeble intellects to conceive of Him who is perfect in all His works,—perfect in the greatest as well as perfect in the smallest,—perfect in appointing the days and hours in which Jupiter, with all his satellites, shall travel round the sun,—perfect in forming the smallest insect that creeps over a few feet of our little globe! How little can our busy helplessness comprehend a Being who is ever ordering all things in heaven and earth by universal providence,—ordering the rise and fall of nations and dynasties, like Nineveh and Carthage;—ordering the exact length to which men like Alexander, and Tamerlane, and Napoleon shall extend their conquests,—ordering the least step in the life of the humblest believer among His people,—all at the same time,—all unceasingly,—all perfectly,—all for His own glory!

The blind man is no judge of the paintings of Rubens or Titian. The deaf man is insensible to the beauty of Handel's music. The Greenlander can have but a faint notion of the climate of the tropics. The Australian savage can form but a remote conception of a locomotive engine, however well you may describe it. There is no place in their minds to take in these things. They have no set of thoughts which can comprehend them. They have no mental fingers to grasp them. And just in the same way, the best and brightest ideas that man can form of God, compared with the reality which we shall see one day, are weak and faint indeed.

But, Reader, one thing, I think, is very clear, and that is this. The more any man considers calmly what God really is, the more he must feel the immeasurable distance between God and himself. The more he meditates, the more he must see that there is a great gulf between him and God. His conscience, I think, will tell him, if he will let it speak, that God is perfect, and he imperfect;—that God is very high, and he very low;— that God is glorious Majesty, and he a poor worm;— and that if ever he is to stand before Him in judgment with comfort, he must have some mighty Helper, or he will not be saved.

And what is all this but the very doctrine of our text? What is all this but coming round to the conclusion I am urging upon you? With such an one as God to give account to, we must have a mighty Saviour. To give us peace with such a glorious Being as God, we must have an Almighty Friend and Advocate on our side,—an Advocate who can answer every charge that can be laid against us, and plead our cause with God on equal terms. We want this, and nothing less than this. Vague notions of mercy will never give true peace. And such a Saviour, such a Friend, such an Advocate is nowhere to be found, excepting in the person of Jesus Christ.

I lay this reason also before you. I know well that people may have false notions of God, as well as everything else, and shut their eyes against truth. But I say boldly and confidently, no man can have really high and honorable views of what God is, and escape the conclusion that the doctrine of our text must be true. There can be no possible salvation, but by Jesus Christ.

3. Let me say, in the third place, this doctrine must be true, *because the Bible is what the Bible is*.

All through the Bible, from Genesis down to Revelation, there is only one simple account of the way in which men must be saved. It is always the same,—only for the sake of our Lord Jesus Christ,—through faith,—not for our own works and deservings.

You see it dimly revealed at first. It looms through the mist of a few promises, but there it is.

You have it more plainly afterwards. It is taught by the pictures and emblems of the law of Moses, the schoolmaster dispensation. (Gal. iii. 24.)

You have it still more clearly by-and-by. The Prophets saw in vision many particulars about the Redeemer yet to come.

You have it fully at last, in the sunshine of the New Testament history,—Christ incarnate,—Christ crucified,—Christ rising again,—Christ preached to the world.

But one golden chain runs through the whole volume,—no salvation excepting by Jesus Christ. The bruising of the serpent's head, foretold in the day of the fall,—the clothing of our first parents with skins,— the sacrifices of Noah, Abraham, Isaac, and Jacob,—the passover, and all the particulars of the Jewish law,— the high-priest,—the altar,—the daily offering of the lamb,—the holy of holies entered only by blood,—the scapegoat,—the cities of refuge,—all are so many witnesses to the truth set forth in the text,—all preach with one voice, salvation only by Jesus Christ.

In fact this truth appears to me the grand subject of the Bible, and all the different parts and portions of the Book are meant to throw light upon it. I can gather from it no ideas of pardon and peace with God, excepting in connection with this truth. If I could read of one soul in it, who was saved without faith in a Saviour, I might perhaps not speak so confidently. But I see that faith in Christ,—whether a coming Christ, or a crucified Christ,—was the prominent feature in the religion of all who went to heaven. I see Abel owning Christ in his better sacrifice at one end of the Bible, and the saints in glory in John's vision, rejoicing in Christ at the other end of the Bible. I see a man like Cornelius, who was devout and feared God, and gave alms, and prayed, not told that he had done all, and would of course be saved, but ordered to send for Peter, and hear of Christ. And when I see all these facts, I feel bound to believe that the doctrine of the text is the doctrine of the whole Bible,—no salvation, no way to heaven excepting by Jesus Christ.

Reader, I do not know what use you make of your Bible,—whether you read it, or whether you do not,—

whether you read it all, or whether you only read such parts as you like. But this I tell you plainly, if you read and believe the whole Bible, you will find it hard to escape the doctrine of the eighteenth Article of the Church of England already quoted. I do not see how you can consistently reject what I have been endeavoring to prove.—Christ is the way,—and the only way,—Christ the truth, and the only truth,—Christ the life, and the only life.

Such are the reasons which seem to me to confirm the truth laid down in our text. What man is,—what God is,—what the Bible is;—all appear to me to lead us on to the same great conclusion,—no possible salvation without Christ. I leave them with you, and pass on.

III. And now, in the third and last place, *let me show you some consequences which flow naturally out of our text.*

There are few parts of this subject which seem to me more important than this. The truth I have been trying to set before you, bears so strongly on the condition of a great proportion of mankind, that I consider it would be mere affectation on my part, not to say something about it. If Christ is the only way of salvation, what are we to feel about many people in the world? This is the point I am now going to take up.

I believe that many persons will go with me so far as I have gone, and would go no further. They will allow my premises. They will have nothing to say to my conclusions. They think it uncharitable to say anything which appears to condemn others. For my part I cannot understand such charity. It seems to me the kind of charity which would see a neighbor drinking slow poison, but never interfere to stop him;—which would allow emigrants to embark in a leaky, ill-found vessel, and not interfere to prevent them;—which would see a blind man walking near a precipice, and think it wrong to cry out and tell him there was danger.

I believe the greatest charity is to tell the greatest quantity of truth. I believe it is no charity to hide the legitimate consequences of such a text as we are now considering, or to shut our eyes against them. And I solemnly call on every one who really believes there is no salvation in any but Christ,—and none other name given under heaven whereby we must be saved,—I solemnly call on that person to listen to me, while I set before him some of the tremendous consequences which the text involves.

I am not going to speak of the heathen, who have never heard the Gospel. Their final state is a great depth, which the mightiest minds have been unable to fathom. I am not ashamed of leaving it alone. One thing only I will say,—if any of the heathen, who die heathen, are saved, I believe they will owe their salvation, however little they may know it on this side of the grave, to the work and atonement of Christ. Just as infants and idiots among ourselves will find in the last day they owed all to Christ, though they never knew Him, so I believe it will be with the heathen, if any of them are saved, whether many or few. For this I am sure of, there is no such thing as creature merit. My own private opinion is, that the highest archangel, (though of course in a very different way and degree from us,) will be found in some way to own his standing to Christ, and that things in heaven, as well as things on earth, will ultimately be found all indebted to the name of Jesus. But I leave the case of the heathen to others, and will speak of matters nearer home.

One mighty consequence then which seems to be learned from this text, is *the utter uselessness of any religion without Christ*.

There are many to be found in Christendom at this day, who have a religion of this kind. They would not like to be called Deists, but Deists they are. That there is a God,—that there is what they are pleased to call

Providence,—that God is merciful,—that there will be a state after death,—this is about the sum and substance of their creed. And as to the distinguishing tenets of Christianity, they do not seem to recognize them at all. Now I denounce such a system as a baseless fabric,— its seeming foundation man's fancy,—its hopes, an utter delusion. The god of such people is an idol of their own invention, and not the glorious God of the Scriptures,—a miserably imperfect being, even on their own showing,—without holiness, without justice, without any attribute but that of vague indiscriminate mercy. Such a religion may possibly do as a toy to live with;— it is far too unreal to die with. It utterly fails to meet the wants of man's conscience. It offers no remedy. It affords no rest for the soles of our feet. It cannot comfort, for it cannot save. Reader, beware of it, if you love life. *Beware of a religion without Christ*.

Another consequence to be learned from the text is, the *folly of any religion in which Christ has not the first place*.

I need not remind you how many hold a system of this kind. The Socinian tells us that Christ was a mere man; that his blood had no more efficacy than that of another; that His death on the cross was not a real atonement and propitiation for man's sins; and that after all doing is the way to heaven, and not believing. I solemnly declare that I believe such a system is ruinous to men's souls. It seems to me to strike at the root of the whole plan of salvation which God has revealed in the Bible, and practically to nullify the greater part of the Scriptures. It overthrows the priesthood of the Lord Jesus, and strips Him of His office. It converts the whole system of the law of Moses touching sacrifices and ordinances, into a meaningless form. It seems to say that the sacrifice of Cain was just as good as the sacrifice of Abel. It turns man adrift on a sea of uncertainty, by plucking from under him the finished work of a divine

Mediator. Beware of it, Reader, no less than of Deism, if you love life. Beware of the least attempt to depreciate and undervalue Christ's person, offices, or work. The name whereby alone you and I can be saved, is a name above every name, and the slightest contempt poured upon it is an insult to the King of kings. The salvation of your soul has been laid by God the Father on Christ, and no other; and if He were not very God of very God, He never could accomplish it,—there could be no salvation at all.

Another consequence to be learned from our text is, the *great error committed by those who add anything to Christ, as necessary to salvation.*

It is an easy thing to profess belief in the Trinity, and reverence for our Lord Jesus Christ, and yet to make some addition to Christ, as the ground of hope, and so to overthrow the doctrine of the text as really and completely as by denying it altogether.

The Church of Rome does this systematically. She adds things over and above the requirements of the Gospel, of her own invention. She speaks as if Christ's finished work was not a sufficient foundation for a sinner's soul; and as if it was not enough to say, "Believe on the Lord Jesus Christ, and thou shalt be saved." She sends men to penances and absolution, to masses and extreme unction, to fasting and bodily mortification, to the Virgin and the saints,—as if these things could add to the safety there is in Christ Jesus. And in doing this she sins against our text with a high hand. Let us beware of any Romish hankering after additions to the simple way of the Gospel, from whatever quarter it may come.

But I fear the Church of Rome does not stand alone in this matter. I fear there are thousands of professing Protestants, who are often erring in the same direction, although of course in a very different degree. They get into a way of adding, perhaps insensibly, other names to the name of Christ, or attaching an importance to them which they never ought to receive. The ultra Churchman in England, who thinks God's covenanted mercies are tied to episcopacy,—the ultra Presbyterian in Scotland, who cannot reconcile prelacy with an intelligent knowledge of the Gospel,—the ultra Free-kirk man by his side, who seems to think lay patronage and vital Christianity almost incompatible,—the ultra Dissenter, who traces every evil in the Church to its connection with the state, and can talk of nothing but the voluntary system,—the ultra Baptist, who shuts out from the Lord's table every one who has not received his views of adult baptism,—the ultra Plymouth Brother, who believes all knowledge to reside with his own body, and condemns every one outside as a poor weak babe;—all these, I say, however unwittingly, appear to me to have a most uncomfortable tendency to add to the doctrine of our text. All seem to me to be practically declaring that salvation is not to be found simply and solely in Christ. All seem to me to be practically adding another name to the name of Jesus whereby men must be saved, even the name of their own party and sect. All seem to me to be practically replying to the question, "What shall I do to be saved?" not merely, "Believe on the Lord Jesus Christ," but also, *"Come and join us."*

Now I call upon every true Christian to beware of such ultraism, in whatsoever form he may be inclined to it. In saying this, I would not be misunderstood. I like every one to be decided in his views of ecclesiastical matters, and to be fully persuaded of their correctness. All I ask is, that you will not put these things in the place of Christ, or place them anywhere near Him, or speak of them as if you thought them needful to salvation. However dear to us our own peculiar views may be, let us beware of thrusting them in between the sinner and the Saviour. Let us beware, in short, of adding to the doctrine of the text. In the things of God's word, be it remembered, addition, as well as subtraction, is a great sin.

The last consequence which seems to me to be learned from our text is, *the utter absurdity of supposing that we ought to be satisfied with a man's state of soul if he is only sincere.*

This is a very common heresy indeed, and one against which we all need to be on our guard. There are thousands who say, in the present day, "We have nothing to do with the opinions of others. They may perhaps be mistaken, though it is possible they are right and we are wrong;—but if they are *sincere* we hope they will be saved, even as we." And all this sounds liberal and charitable, and people like to fancy their own views are so.

Now, I believe such notions are entirely contradictory to the Bible, whatever else they may be. I cannot find in Scripture that any one ever got to heaven merely by sincerity, or was accepted with God if he was only earnest in maintaining his own views. The priests of Baal were sincere when they cut themselves with knives and lancets till the blood gushed out; but still that did not prevent Elijah from commanding them to be treated as wicked idolaters. Manasseh, king of Judah, was doubtless sincere when he burned his children in the fire to Moloch; but who does not know that he brought on himself great guilt by so doing? The Apostle Paul, when a Pharisee, was sincere while he made havoc of the Church; but when his eyes were opened he mourned over this as a special wickedness. Let us beware of allowing for a moment, that sincerity is everything, and that we have no right to think ill of a man's spiritual state, because of the opinions he holds, if he is only earnest in holding them. On such principles the Druidical sacrifices, the car of Juggernaut, the Indian Suttees, the systematic murders of the Thugs, the fires of Smithfield, might each and all be defended. It will not stand. It will not bear the test of Scripture. Once allow such notions to be true, and you may as well throw your Bible aside altogether. *Sincerity is not Christ*, and therefore sincerity cannot put away sin.

I dare be sure these consequences sound very unpleasant to the minds of some who may read them. But I tell you of them advisedly and deliberately. I say calmly that a religion without Christ,—a religion that takes away from Christ,—a religion that adds anything to Christ,—a religion that puts sincerity in the place of Christ,—all are dangerous,—all are to be avoided, and all are alike contrary to the doctrine of our text.

You may not like this. I am sorry for it. You think me uncharitable,—illiberal,—narrow-minded,—bigoted, and so forth. Be it so. But you will not tell me my doctrine is not that of the word of God, and of the Church of England, whose minister I am. That Doctrine is salvation in Christ to the very uttermost,—but out of Christ no salvation at all.

I feel it a duty to bear my solemn testimony against the spirit of the day you live in; to warn you against its infection. It is not Atheism I fear so much in the present times as Pantheism. It is not the system which says nothing is true, so much as the system which says *everything is true*. It is not the system which says there is no Saviour, so much as the system which says there are many Saviours, and many ways to peace. It is the system which is so liberal, that it dares not say anything is false. It is the system which is so charitable, that it will allow everything to be true. It is the system which seems ready to allow honor to others as well as our Lord Jesus Christ, and to hope well of all men, however contradictory their religious opinions may be. Confucius and Zoroaster,—Socrates and Mahomet,—the Indian Brahmins and the African devil-worshippers,—Arius and Pelagius,—Ignatius Loyola and Socinus, all are to be treated respectfully, none are to be condemned. It is the system which bids us smile complacently on all the creeds and systems of religion,—the Bible and the Koran,—the Hindoo Vedas and the Persian Zendavesta,—the old wives' fables of Rabbinical writers and the rubbish of Patristic traditions,—the Racovian Catechism and the Thirty-nine Articles,—the Revelations of Emanuel Swedenborg and the Book of Mormon of Joseph Smith;—all are to be listened to, none are to be denounced as lies. It is the system which is so scrupulous about the feelings of others, that we are never to say they are wrong. It is the system which is so liberal, that it calls a man a bigot, if he dares to say, "I know my views are right." This is the system, this is the tone of feeling which I fear in this day. This is the system which I desire emphatically to testify against and denounce.

What is it but a bowing down before a great idol, speciously called liberality? What is it all but a sacrificing of truth upon the altar of a caricature of charity? Beware of it, Reader,—beware that the rushing stream of public opinion does not carry you away. Beware of it, if you believe the Bible. Beware of it, if you are a consistent member of the Church of England. Has the Lord God spoken to us in the Bible, or has He not? Has He shown us the way of salvation plainly in that Bible, or has He not? Has He declared to us the dangerous state of all out of that way, or has He not? Gird up the loins of your mind, and look these questions fairly in the face, and give them an honest answer. Tell us that there is some other inspired book beside the Bible, and then we shall know what you mean. Tell us that the whole Bible is not inspired, and then we shall know where to meet you. But grant for a moment that the Bible, the whole Bible, and nothing but the Bible is God's truth, and then I know not in what way you can escape the doctrine of the text. From the liberality which says everybody is right,—from the charity which forbids you to say anybody is wrong,—from the peace which is bought at the expense of truth, may the good Lord deliver you!

I speak for myself.—I find no resting-place between downright evangelical Christianity and downright infidelity—whatever others may find. I see no half-way house between them, or houses that are roofless and cannot shelter my weary soul. I can see consistency in an infidel, however much I may pity him. I can see consistency in the full maintenance of evangelical truth. But as to a middle course between the two, I cannot see it, and I say so plainly. Let it be called illiberal and uncharitable, I can hear God's voice nowhere except in the Bible, and I can see no salvation for sinners in the Bible excepting through Jesus Christ. In Him I see abundance. Out of Him I see none. And as for those who hold religions in which Christ is not all, whoever they may be, I have a most uncomfortable feeling about their safety. I do not for a moment say that none of them are saved, but I say that those who are saved are saved by their disagreement with their own principles, and in spite of their own system. The man who wrote the famous line,

"He can't be wrong whose life is in the right,

was a great poet, undoubtedly, but he was a wretched divine.

Let me conclude with a few words, by way of application.

First of all, if there is no salvation excepting in Christ, make sure that you have an interest in that salvation yourself. Do not be content with hearing and approving, and assenting to the truth, and go no further. Seek to have a personal interest in this salvation. Lay hold by faith for your own soul. Rest not till you know and feel that you have got actual possession of that peace with God, which Jesus offers, and that Christ is yours and you are Christ's. If there were two or three or more ways of getting to heaven, there would be no necessity for pressing this matter upon you. But if there is *only one way* you will hardly wonder that I say "make sure that you are in it."

Secondly, if there is no salvation excepting in Christ, try to do good to the souls of all who do not know Him as a Saviour. There are millions in this miserable condition,—millions in foreign lands,—millions in your own country,—millions who are not trusting in Christ. You ought to feel for them, if you are a true Christian;—you ought to pray for them;—you ought to work for them, while there is yet time. Do you really believe that Christ is the only way to heaven?—then live as if you believed it.

Look round the circle of your own relatives and friends. Count them up one by one, and think how many of them are not yet in Christ. Try to do good to them in some way or other. Act as a man should act who believes his friends to be in danger. Do not be content with their being kind and amiable, gentle and good-tempered, moral and courteous,—be miserable about them till they come to Christ, and trust in Him,— for miserable you ought to be. Let nobody alone who is out of Christ, if only you have opportunities of reaching him. I know all this may sound like enthusiasm and fanaticism. I wish there was more of it in the world. Anything, I am sure, is better than a quiet indifference about the souls of others, as if everybody was in the way to heaven. Nothing, to my mind, so proves our little faith, as our little feeling about the spiritual condition of those around us.

Thirdly, if there is no salvation excepting in Christ, let us love all who love the Lord Jesus in sincerity and exalt Him as their Saviour, whoever they may be. Let us not draw back and look shy on others, because they do not see eye to eye with ourselves in everything. Whether a man be a Free-kirk-man or an Independent, a Wesleyan or a Baptist, let us love him if he loves Christ, and gives Christ His rightful place. We are all fast travelling towards a place where names and forms and Church-government will be nothing, and Christ will be all. Let us get ready for that place betimes, by loving all who are in the way that leads to it.

This is the true charity, to believe all things, and hope all things, so long as we see Bible doctrines maintained, and Christ exalted. Christ must be the single standard by which all opinions must be measured. Let us honor all who honor Him. But let us never forget that the same Apostle Paul who wrote about charity, says also, "If any man love not the Lord Jesus Christ, let him be Anathema." (1 Cor. xvi. 22.) If our charity and liberality are wider than that of the Bible, they are worth nothing at all. Indiscriminate love is no love at all, and indiscriminate approbation of all religious opinions, is only a new name for infidelity. Let us hold out the right hand to all who love the Lord Jesus, but let us beware how we go beyond this.

Lastly, if there is no salvation excepting by Christ, you must not be surprised if ministers of the Gospel preach much about Him. We cannot tell you too much about the Name which is above every name. You cannot hear of Him too often. You may hear too much about controversy in our sermons,—you may hear too much of men and books, of works and duties, of forms and ceremonies, of sacraments and ordinances. But there is one subject which you never hear too much of,—you can never hear too much of Christ.

When we are wearied of preaching Him, we are false ministers. When you are wearied of hearing of Him, your souls are in an unhealthy state. When we have preached Him all our lives, the half of His excellence will remain untold. When you see Him face to face in the day of His appearing, you will find there was more in Him than your heart ever conceived.

Let me leave you with the words of an old writer, to which I desire humbly to subscribe:—"I know no true religion but Christianity; no true Christianity but the doctrine of Christ,—the doctrine of His divine person, of His divine office, of His divine righteousness, and of His divine Spirit, which all that are His receive. I know no true ministers of Christ, but such as make it their business, in their calling, to commend Jesus Christ, in His saving fulness of grace and glory, to the faith and love of men;—no true Christian but one united to Christ by faith and love, unto the glorifying of the name of Jesus Christ in the beauty of Gospel holiness. Ministers and Christians of this spirit have been for many years my brethren and companions, and I hope shall ever be, whithersoever the hand of God shall lead me."

VI. CHRIST AND THE TWO THIEVES

> *"And one of the malefactors which were hanged railed on him, saying, if thou be Christ, save thyself and us. But the other answering rebuked him, saying, dost not thou fear God, seeing thou art in the same condemnation? And we indeed justly: for we receive the due reward of our deeds: but this man hath done nothing amiss. And he said unto Jesus, Lord, remember me when thou comest into thy kingdom. And Jesus said unto him, verily i say unto thee, to-day shalt thou be with me in paradise."*
>
> LUKE XXIII. 39-43

READER,—

You know these verses, I suppose. It would be strange indeed if you did not. Few passages in the New Testament are more familiar to men's ears.

And it is right and good that these verses should be well known. They have comforted many troubled minds. They have brought peace to many uneasy consciences. They have been a healing balm to many wounded hearts. They have been a medicine to many sin-sick souls. They have smoothed down not a few dying pillows. Wherever the Gospel of Christ is preached, they will always be honored, loved, and had in remembrance.

Reader, I wish to speak to you about these verses. Listen to me while I try to unfold the leading lessons which they are meant to teach. I cannot see the state of your heart before God, but I can see truths in this passage which no man can ever know too well.

I. First of all you are meant to learn from these verses *Christ's power and willingness to save sinners*.

This is the main doctrine to be gathered from the history of the penitent thief. It teaches you that which ought to be music in the ears of all who hear it,—it teaches you that Jesus Christ is mighty to save.

I ask you if any man's case could look more hopeless and desperate, than that of this penitent thief once did?

He was a *wicked man*—a malefactor,—a thief, if not a murderer. We know this, for such only were crucified. He was suffering a just punishment for breaking the laws. And as he had lived wicked, so he seemed determined to die wicked,—for when he first was crucified he railed on our Lord.

And he was a *dying man*. He hung there, nailed to a cross, from which he was never to come down alive. He had no longer power to stir hand or foot. His hours were numbered. The grave was ready for him. There was but a step between him and death.

If ever there was a soul hovering on the brink of hell, it was the soul of this thief. If ever there was a case that seemed lost, gone, and past recovery, it was his. If ever there was a child of Adam whom the devil made sure of as his own, it was this man.

But see now what happened. He ceased to rail and blaspheme, as he had done at the first. He began to speak in another manner altogether. He turned to our blessed Lord in prayer. He prayed Jesus to "remember him when He came into His kingdom." He asked that his soul might be cared for, his sins pardoned, and himself thought of in another world. Truly this was a wonderful change.

And then mark what kind of answer he received. Some would have said he was too wicked a man to be saved. But it was not so. Some would have fancied it was too late, the door was shut, and there was no room for mercy. But it proved not too late at all. The Lord Jesus returned him an immediate answer,—spoke kindly to him,—assured him he should be with Him that day in paradise,—pardoned him completely—cleansed him thoroughly from his sins—received him graciously—justified him freely—raised him from the gates of hell,—gave him a title to glory. Of all the multitude of saved souls, none ever received so glorious an assurance of his own salvation, as did this penitent thief. Go over the whole list from Genesis to Revelation, and you will find none who had such words spoken to them as these, "To-day shalt thou be with me in paradise."

Reader, the Lord Jesus never gave so complete a proof of His power and will to save, as He did upon this occasion. In the day when He seemed most weak, He showed that he was a strong deliverer. In the hour when his body was racked with pain, He showed that He could feel tenderly for others. At the time when He Himself was dying, he conferred on a sinner eternal life.

Now have I not a right to say, "Jesus is able to save to the uttermost all them that come unto God through Him?" Behold the proof of it. If ever sinner was too far gone to be saved, it was this thief. Yet he was plucked as a brand from the fire.

Have I not a right to say. "Christ will receive any poor sinner who comes to Him with the prayer of faith, and cast out none?" Behold the proof of it. If ever there was one that seemed too bad to be received, this was the man. Yet the door of mercy was wide open even for him.

Have I not a right to say, "By grace ye may be saved through faith, not of works,—fear not, only believe?" Behold the proof of it. This thief was never baptized. He belonged to no visible church. He never received the Lord's Supper. He never did any work for Christ. He never gave money to Christ's cause,—But he had *faith*, and so he was saved.

Have I not a right to say, "The youngest faith will save a man's soul, if it only be true?" Behold the proof of it. This man's faith was only one day old, but it led him to Christ, and preserved him from hell.

Why then should any man or woman despair with such a passage as this in the Bible? Jesus is a physician who can cure hopeless cases. He can quicken dead souls, and call the things which be not as though they were.

Never should any man or woman despair! Jesus is still the same now that He was eighteen hundred years ago. The keys of death and hell are in His hand. When He opens none can shut.[38]

What though your sins be more in number than the hairs of your head? What though your evil habits have grown with your growth, and strengthened with your strength? What though you have hitherto hated good, and loved evil, all the days of your life? These things are sad indeed; but there is hope even for you. Christ can heal you. Christ can cleanse you. Christ can raise you from your low estate. Heaven is not shut against you. Christ is able to admit you, if you will humbly commit your soul into His hands.

Reader, *are your sins forgiven?* If not, I set before you this day a full and free salvation. I invite you to follow the steps of the penitent thief,—come to Christ, and live. I tell you that Jesus is very pitiful, and of tender mercy. I tell you He can do everything that your soul requires. Though your sins be as scarlet, He can make them white as snow; though they be red like crimson, they shall be as wool. Why should you not be saved as well as another? Come unto Christ by faith, and live.

---

38 "O Saviour, what a precedent is this of thy free and powerful grace! Where thou wilt give, what unworthiness can bar us from thy mercy? When thou wilt give, what time can prejudice our vocation? Who can despair of thy goodness when he, that in the morning was posting to hell, is in the evening with thee in paradise?"—*Bishop Hall.*

Reader, *are you a true believer?* If you are, you ought to glory in Christ. Glory not in your own faith, your own feelings, your own knowledge, your own prayers, your own amendment, your own diligence. Glory in nothing but Christ. Alas! the best of us knows but little of that merciful and mighty Saviour. We do not exalt Him and glory in Him enough. Let us pray that we may see more of the fulness there is in Him.

Reader, *do you ever try to do good to others?* If you do, remember to tell them about Christ. Tell the young, tell the poor, tell the aged, tell the ignorant, tell the sick, tell the dying,—tell them all about Christ. Tell them of His power, and tell them of His love. Tell them of His doings, and tell them of His feelings. Tell them of what He has done for the chief of sinners. Tell them what He is willing to do to the last day of time. Tell it them over and over again. Never be tired of speaking of Christ. Say to them broadly and fully, freely and unconditionally, unreservedly and undoubtingly, "Come unto Christ as the penitent thief did,—come unto Christ, and you shall be saved."

II. The second lesson you are meant to learn from this passage is this, *If some are saved in the very hour of death, others are not.*

This is a truth that never ought to be passed over, and I dare not leave it unnoticed. It is a truth that stands out plainly in the sad end of the other malefactor, and is only too often forgotten.

What became of the other thief who was crucified? Why did he not turn from sin, and call upon the Lord? Why did he remain hardened and impenitent? Why was he not saved? It is useless to try to answer such questions. Let us be content to take the fact as we find it, and see what it is meant to teach us.

We have no right whatever to say this thief was a worse man than his companion. There is nothing to prove it. Both plainly were wicked men. Both were receiving the due reward of their deeds. Both hung by the side of our Lord Jesus Christ. Both heard Him pray for His murderers. Both saw Him suffer patiently. But while one repented, the other remained hardened. While one began to pray, the other went on railing. While one was converted in his last hours, the other died a bad man as he had lived. While one was taken to paradise, the other went to his own place, the place of the devil and his angels.

Now these things are written for our warning. There is warning as well as comfort in these verses, and that very solemn warning too.

They tell me loudly, that though some may repent and be converted on their death-beds, it does not at all follow that all will. A death-bed is not always a saving time.

They tell me loudly, that two men may have the same opportunities of getting good for their souls, may be placed in the same position, see the same things, and hear the same things,—and yet only one shall take advantage of them, repent, believe, and be saved.

They tell me, above all, that repentance and faith are the gifts of God, and are not in a man's own power; and that if any one flatters himself he can repent at his own time, choose his own season, seek the Lord when he please, and, like the penitent thief, be saved at the very last,—he may find at length that he is greatly deceived.

And it is good and profitable to bear this in mind. There is an immense amount of delusion in the world on this very subject. I see many allowing life to slip away, all unprepared to die. I see many allowing that they ought to repent, but always putting off their own repentance. And I believe one grand reason is, that most men suppose they can turn to God just when they like. They wrest the parable of the laborer in the vineyard, which speaks of the eleventh hour, and use it as it never was meant to be used. They dwell on the pleasant part of the verses I am now considering, and forget the rest. They talk of the thief that went to paradise, and was saved, and forget the one who died as he had lived, — and was lost.[39]

Reader, take heed that you do not fall into this mistake. Look at the history of men in the Bible, and see how often these notions I have been speaking of are contradicted. Mark well how many proofs there are that two men may have the same light offered them, and only one use it; and that no one has a right to take liberties with God's mercy, and presume he will be able to repent just when he likes.

Look at Saul and David. They lived about the same time. They rose from the same rank in life. They were called to the same position in the world. They enjoyed the ministry of the same prophet, Samuel. They reigned the same number of years. — Yet one was saved, and the other lost.

Look at Sergius Paulus and Gallio. They were both Roman governors. They were both wise and prudent men in their generation. They both heard the Apostle Paul preach. But one believed, and was baptized, — the other "cared for none of these things." (Acts xviii. 17.)

Look at the world around you. See what is going on continually under your eyes. Two sisters will often

---

39 "He that puts off his repentance and seeking for pardon to the very last, in reliance upon this example, does but tempt God, and turn that to his own poison which God intended for better ends." "The mercies of God are never recorded in Scripture for man's presumption, and the failings of men never for imitation." — *Lightfoot. Sermon*. 1684.

"Most ungrateful and foolish is the conduct of those who take encouragement from the penitent thief to put off repentance to a dying moment; — most ungrateful in perverting the grace of their Redeemer into an occasion of renewing their provocations against Him; — and most foolish to imagine that what our Lord did in so singular circumstances, is to be drawn into an ordinary precedent." — *Doddridge*.

attend the same ministry, listen to the same truths, hear the same sermons; and yet only one shall be converted to God, while the other remains totally unmoved. Two friends often read the same religious book. One is so moved by it, that he gives up all for Christ: the other sees nothing at all in it, and continues the same as before. Hundreds have read Doddridge's Rise and Progress without profit. With Wilberforce it was one of the beginnings of spiritual life. Thousands have read Wilberforce's Practical View of Christianity, and laid it down again unaltered;—from the time Legh Richmond read it he became another man. No man has any warrant for saying, Salvation is in my own power.

Reader, I do not pretend to explain these things. I only put them before you as great facts. And I ask you to consider them well.

You must not misunderstand me. I do not want to discourage you. I say these things in all affection to give you warning of danger. I do not say them to drive you back from heaven;—I say them rather to draw you on, and bring you to Christ while He can be found.

I want you to beware of presumption. Do not abuse God's mercy and compassion. Do not continue in sin, I beseech you, and think you can repent, and believe, and be saved, just when you like, when you please, when you will, and when you choose. I would always set before you an open door. I would always say, while there is life there is hope. But if you would be wise, put nothing off that concerns your soul.

I want you to beware of letting slip good thoughts and godly convictions, if you have them. Cherish them and nourish them, lest you lose them forever. Make the most of them, lest they take to themselves wings and flee away. Have you an inclination to begin praying? Put it in practice at once. Have you an idea of beginning really to serve Christ? Set about it at once. Are you enjoying any spiritual light? See that you live up to your light. Trifle not with opportunities, lest the day come when you will want to use them, and not be able. Linger not, lest you become wise too late.

You may say, perhaps, "It is never too late to repent." I answer, That is right enough but late repentance is seldom true. And I say further, you cannot be certain if you put off repenting, you will repent at all.

You may say, "Why should I be afraid? — the penitent thief was saved." I answer, That is true, but look again at the passage, which tells you that the other thief was lost.

III. The third lesson you are meant to learn from these verses is this; *the Spirit always leads saved souls in one way*.

This is a point that deserves particular attention, and is often overlooked. Men look at the broad fact that the penitent thief was saved when he was dying, and they look no further.

They do not consider the evidences this thief left behind him. They do not observe the abundant proofs he gave of the work of the Spirit in his heart. And these proofs I wish to trace out. I wish to show you that the Spirit always works in one way, and that whether He converts a man in an hour — as He did the penitent thief — or whether by slow degrees, as he does others, the steps by which He leads souls to heaven are always the same.

Listen to me, Reader, and I will try to make this clear to you. I want you to shake off the common notion, that there is some easy royal road to heaven from a dying-bed. I want you thoroughly to understand that every saved soul goes through the same experience, and that the leading principles of the penitent thief's religion were just the same as those of the oldest saint that ever lived.

See then, for one thing, *how strong was the faith* of this man.

He called Jesus, "Lord." He declared his belief that he would have a kingdom. He believed that He was able to give him eternal life and glory, and in this belief prayed to Him. He maintained His innocence of all the charges brought against Him: "This man," said he, "hath done nothing amiss." Others perhaps may have *thought* the Lord innocent,—none *said* so openly but this poor dying man.

And when did all this happen? It happened when the whole nation had denied Christ,—shouting, "Crucify him, crucify him; we have no king but Cæsar,"—when the chief priests and pharisees had condemned and found Him guilty of death,—when even His own disciples had forsaken Him and fled,—when He was hanging, faint, bleeding, and dying on the cross, numbered with transgressors, and counted accursed. This was the hour when the thief believed in Christ, and prayed to Him. Surely such faith was never seen since the world began.[40]

---

40 "I know not that since the creation of the world there ever was a more remarkable and striking example of faith."—*Calvin's Commentary on the Gospels*.

"A great faith that can see the sun under so thick a cloud; that can discover a Christ, a Saviour, under such a poor, scorned, despised, crucified Jesus, and call him Lord.

"A great faith that could see Christ's kingdom through His cross, and grave, and death, and when there was so little sign of a kingdom, and pray to be remembered in that kingdom."—*Lightfoot. Sermon.* 1684.

"The penitent thief was the first confessor of Christ's heavenly kingdom,—the first martyr who bore testimony to the holiness of His sufferings,—and the first apologist for His oppressed innocence."—*Quesnel on the Gospels*.

"Probably there are few saints in glory who ever honored Christ more illustriously than this dying sinner."—*Doddridge*.

"Is this the voice of a thief or a disciple? Give me leave, O Saviour, to borrow thine own words, 'Verily I have not found so great faith, no not in Israel.' He saw thee hanging miserably by him, and yet styles thee Lord. He saw thee dying, and yet talks of thy kingdom. He felt himself dying, yet talks of a future remem-

The disciples had seen mighty signs and miracles. They had seen the dead raised with a word, and lepers healed with a touch,—the blind receiving sight,—the dumb made to speak,—the lame made to walk. They had seen thousands fed with a few loaves and fishes. They had seen their Master walking on the water as on dry land. They had all of them heard Him speak as no man ever spake, and hold out promises of good things yet to come. They had some of them had a foretaste of His glory in the mount of transfiguration. Doubtless their faith was the gift of God, but still they had much to help it.

The dying thief saw none of the things I have mentioned. He only saw our Lord in agony, and in weakness, in suffering and in pain. He saw Him undergoing a dishonorable punishment, deserted, mocked, despised, blasphemed. He saw Him rejected by all the great, and wise, and noble of His own people,—His strength dried up like a potsherd, his life drawing to the grave. (Psalm xxii. 15, lxxxviii. 3.) He saw no sceptre, no royal crown, no outward dominion, no glory, no majesty, no power, no signs of might. And yet the dying thief believed and looked forward to Christ's kingdom.

Reader, would you know if you have the Spirit? Then mark the question I put to you this day:—Where is your faith in Christ?

See, for another thing, *what a right sense of sin* the thief had. He says to his companion, "We receive the due reward of our deeds." He acknowledges his own ungodliness, and the justice of his punishment. He makes no attempt to justify himself, or excuse his wickedness. He speaks like a man humbled and self-abased by the remembrance of past iniquities. This is what all

---

brance. O faith, stronger than death, which can look beyond the cross at a crown;—beyond dissolution at a remembrance of life and glory! Which of thine eleven were heard to speak so gracious a word to thee in these thy last pangs?"—*Bishop Hall.*

God's children feel. They are ready to allow they are poor hell-deserving sinners. They can say with their hearts, as well as with their lips, "We have left undone the things that we ought to have done, and we have done those things that we ought not to have done, and there is no health in us."

Reader, would you know if you had the Spirit? Then mark my question:—Do you feel your sin?

See, for another thing, *what brotherly love* the thief showed to his companion. He tried to stop his railing and blaspheming, and bring him to a better mind. "Dost thou not fear God," he says, "seeing thou art in the same condemnation?" There is no surer mark of grace than this. Grace shakes a man out of his selfishness, and makes him feel for the souls of others. When the Samaritan woman was converted, she left her water pot, and ran to the city, saying, "Come see a man that told me all things that ever I did; is not this the Christ?" (John iv. 29.) When Saul was converted, immediately he went to the synagogue at Damascus, and testified to his brethren of Israel, that Jesus was the Christ. (Acts ix. 20.)

Reader, would you know if you had the Spirit? Then where is your charity and love to souls?

In one word, you see in the penitent thief a finished work of the Holy Ghost. Every part of the believer's character may be traced in him. Short as his life was after conversion, he found time to leave abundant evidence that he was a child of God. His faith,—his prayer,—his humility,—his brotherly love,—are unmistakable witnesses of the reality of his repentance. He was not a penitent in name only, but in deed and in truth.

Let no man therefore think, because the penitent thief was saved, that men can be saved without leaving any evidence of the Spirit's work. Let such an one consider well what evidence this man left behind, and take care.

It is mournful to hear what people sometimes say about what they call *death-bed evidences*. It is perfectly fearful to observe how little satisfies some persons, and how easily they can persuade themselves that their friends are gone to heaven. They will tell you when their relation is dead and gone, that "he made such a beautiful prayer one day,—or that he talked so well,—or that he was so sorry for his old ways, and intended to live so differently if he got better,—or that he craved nothing in this world,—or that he liked people to read to him, and pray with him." And because they have this to go upon they seem to have a comfortable hope that he is saved. Christ may never have been named,—the way of salvation may never have been in the least mentioned. But it matters not; there was a little talk of religion, and so they are content.

Now I have no desire to hurt the feelings of any one who reads this paper, but I must and will speak plainly on this subject.

Once for all let me say that, as a general rule, nothing is so unsatisfactory as death-bed evidences. The things that men say, and the feelings they express when sick and frightened, are little to be depended on. Often, too often, they are the result of fear, and do not spring from the ground of the heart. Often, too often, they are things said by rote, caught from the lips of ministers and anxious friends, but evidently not felt. And nothing can prove all this more clearly than the well-known fact, that the great majority of persons who make promises of amendment on a sick-bed, if they recover, go back to sin and the world.

When a man has lived a life of thoughtlessness and folly, I want something more than a few fair words, and good wishes, to satisfy me about his soul when he comes to his death-bed It is not enough for me that he will let me read the Bible to him, and pray by his bedside; that he says, "he has not thought so much as he ought of religion, and he thinks he should be a different man if he got better." All this does not content me, — it does not make me feel happy about his state. It is very well as far as it goes, but it is not conversion. It is very well in its way, but it is not faith in Christ. Until I see conversion, and faith in Christ, I cannot and dare not feel satisfied. Others may feel satisfied, if they please, and after their friend's death say, they hope he has gone to heaven. For my part I would rather say nothing at all. I would be content with the least measure of repentance and faith in a dying man, even though it were no bigger than a grain of mustard seed; but to be content with anything less than repentance and faith seems to me next door to infidelity.

Reader, what kind of evidence do you mean to leave behind as to the state of your soul? Take example by the penitent thief, and you will do well.

When we have carried you to your narrow bed, let us not have to hunt up stray words, and scraps of religion, in order to make out that you were a true believer. Let us not have to say in a hesitating way one to another, "I trust he is happy, he talked so nicely one day, and he seemed so pleased with a chapter in the Bible on another occasion, and he liked such a person who is a good man." Let us be able to speak decidedly as to your condition. Let us have some standing proof of your penitence, your faith, and your holiness, that none shall be able for a moment to question your state. Depend on it, without this, those you leave behind can feel no solid comfort about your soul. We may use the form of religion at your burial, and express charitable hopes. We may meet you at the church-yard gate, and say, "Blessed are the dead that die in the Lord." But this will not alter your condition. If you die without conversion to God, — without repentance, — and without faith, your funeral will only be the funeral of a lost soul.

IV. You are meant in the next place to learn from these verses that *believers in Christ when they die, are with the Lord.*

This you may gather from our Lord's words to the penitent thief, "This day shalt thou be with me in paradise." And you have an expression very like it in the Epistle to the Philippians, where Paul says he has a desire to "depart and be with Christ." (Phil. i. 23.)

I shall say but little on this subject. I would simply lay it before you for your own private meditations. To my own mind it is very full of comfort and peace.

Believers after death are "with Christ." That answers many a difficult question, which otherwise might puzzle man's busy, restless mind. The abode of dead saints, their joys, their feelings, their happiness, all seems met by this simple expression,—They are with Christ.

I cannot enter into full explanations about the state of departed believers. It is a high and deep subject, such as man's mind can neither grasp nor fathom. I know their happiness falls short of what it will be when their bodies are raised again, and Jesus returns to earth. Yet I know also they enjoy a blessed rest,—a rest from labor,—a rest from sorrow,—a rest from pain,—and a rest from sin. But it does not follow because I cannot explain these things, that I am not persuaded they are far happier than they ever were on earth. I see their happiness in this very passage, "They are with Christ," and when I see that I see enough.

If the sheep are with the Shepherd,—if the members are with the Head,—if the children of Christ's family are with Him who loved them and carried them all the days of their pilgrimage on earth, all must be well, all must be right.

I cannot describe what kind of a place paradise is, but I ask no brighter view of it than this, that Christ is there.[41] All other things in the picture which imagination draws of paradise are nothing in comparison of this. How He is there, and in what way He is there, I know not. Let me only see Christ in paradise when my eyes close in death, and that suffices me. Well does the Psalmist say, "In thy presence is fulness of joy." It was a true saying of a dying girl, when her mother tried to comfort her by describing what paradise would be, "There," she said to the child, "there you will have no pains, and no sickness; there you will see your brothers and sisters who have gone before you, and will be always happy." "Ah! mother," was the reply, "but there is one thing better than all and that is, *Christ will be there.*"

Reader, it may be you do not think much about your soul. It may be you know little of Christ as your Saviour, and have never tasted by experience that He is precious. And yet perhaps you hope to go to paradise when you die. Surely this passage is one that should make you think. Paradise is a place where Christ is. Then can it be a place that you would enjoy?

Reader, it may be you are a believer, and yet tremble at the thought of the grave. It seems cold and dreary. You feel as if all before you was dark, and gloomy, and comfortless. Fear not, but be encouraged by this text. You are going to paradise, and Christ will be there.

V. The last thing you are meant to learn from these verses is this, "*the eternal portion of every man's soul is close to him.*"

"To-day," says our Lord to the penitent thief, "to-day shalt thou be with me in paradise." He names no distant period,—He does not talk of his entering into a

---

41 "We ought not to enter into curious and subtle arguments about the place of paradise. Let us rest satisfied with knowing that those who are engrafted by faith into the body of Christ are partakers of life, and there enjoy after death a blessed and joyful rest, until the perfect glory of the heavenly life is fully manifested by the coming of Christ."—*Calvin's Commentary on the Gospels.*

state of happiness as a thing "far away." He speaks of to-day, "this very day in which thou art hanging on the cross."

Reader, how near that seems! How awfully near that word brings our everlasting dwelling-place.—Happiness or misery,—sorrow or joy,—the presence of Christ, or the company of devils,—all are close to us. "There is but a step," says David, "between me and death." (1 Sam. xx. 3.) There is but a step, we may say, between ourselves and either paradise or hell.

We none of us realize this as we ought to do. It is high time to shake off the dreamy state of mind in which we live on this matter. We are apt to talk or think, even about believers, as if death was a long journey,—as if the dying saint had embarked on a long voyage. It is all wrong, very wrong. Their harbor and their home is close by, and they have entered in.

Some of us know by bitter experience what a long and weary time it is between the death of those we love, and the hour when we bury them out of sight. Such weeks are the slowest, saddest, heaviest weeks in all our lives. But, blessed be God, the souls of departed saints are free from the very moment their last breath is drawn. While we are weeping, and the coffin preparing, and the mourning being provided, and the last painful arrangement being made, the spirits of our beloved ones are enjoying the presence of Christ. They are freed forever from the burden of the flesh. They are where the wicked cease from troubling, and the weary are at rest.

Reader, the day that believers die they are in paradise. Their battle is fought;—their strife is over. They have passed through that gloomy valley we must one day tread;—they have gone over that dark river we must one day cross. They have drank that last bitter cup which sin has mingled for man. They have reached that place where sorrow and sighing are no more. Surely we should not wish them back again. We should not weep for them, but for ourselves.

We are warring still, but they are at peace. We are laboring, but they are at rest. We are watching, but they are sleeping. We are wearing our spiritual armor, but they have forever put it off. We are still at sea, but they are safe in harbor. We have tears, but they have joy. We are strangers and pilgrims, but as for them they are at home. Surely, better are the dead in Christ than the living. Surely the very hour the poor saint dies he is at once higher and happier than the highest upon earth.[42]

I fear there is a vast amount of delusion on this point. I fear that many, who are not Roman Catholics, and profess not to believe in purgatory, have, notwithstanding, some strange ideas in their minds about the immediate consequences of death. I fear that many have a sort of vague notion that there is some interval or space of time between death and their eternal state. They fancy they shall go through a kind of purifying change, and that though they die unfit for heaven, they shall yet be found meet for it after all.

But it will not stand. There is no change after death. There is no conversion in the grave. There is no new heart given after the last breath is drawn. The very day we go we launch for ever. The day we go from this world, we begin an eternal condition. From that day there is no spiritual alteration,—no spiritual change. As we die, so we shall receive after death. As the tree falls, so it must lie.

---

[42] "We give thee hearty thanks, for that it hath pleased thee to deliver this our brother out of the miseries of this sinful world."—*Church of England Burial Service*.

"I have some of the best news to impart. One beloved by you has accomplished her warfare; has received an answer to her prayers, and everlasting joy rests upon her head. My dear wife, the source of my best earthly comfort for twenty years, departed on Tuesday."—*Venn's Letter to Stillingfleet, announcing the death of his wife*.

Reader, if you are an unconverted man, this ought to make you think. Do you know you are close to hell? This very day you might die, and if you died out of Christ, you would open your eyes in hell, and in torment.

Reader, if you are a true Christian, you are far nearer heaven than you think. This very day, if the Lord should take you, you would find yourself in paradise. The good land of promise is near to you. The eyes that you closed in weakness and pain, would open at once on a glorious rest, such as my tongue cannot describe.

And now let me say a few words in conclusion, and I have done.

This tract may fall into the hands of some humble-hearted and contrite sinner.—Are you that man? Then here is encouragement for you. See what the penitent thief did, and do likewise. See how he prayed,—see how he called on the Lord Jesus Christ,—see what an answer of peace he obtained. Brother or sister, why should not you do the same? Why should not you also be saved?

This tract may fall into the hands of some proud and presumptuous man of the world.—Are you that man? Then take warning. See how the impenitent thief died as he had lived, and beware lest you come to a like end. Oh! erring brother or sister, be not too confident, lest you die in your sins. Seek the Lord while He may be found. Turn you, turn, why will you die?

This tract may fall into the hands of some professing believer in Christ.—Are you such an one? Then take the penitent thief's religion as a measure by which to prove your own. See that you know something of true repentance and saving faith, of real humility and fervent charity. Brother or sister, do not be satisfied with the world's standard of Christianity. Be of one mind with the penitent thief, and you will be wise.

This tract may fall into the hands of some one who is mourning over departed believers. Are you such an one? Then take comfort from this Scripture. See how your beloved ones are in the best of hands. They cannot be better off. They never were so well in their lives as they are now. They are with Jesus, whom their souls loved on earth. Oh! cease from your selfish mourning. Rejoice rather that they are freed from trouble, and have entered into rest.

And this tract may fall into the hands of some aged servant of Christ.—Are you such an one? Then see from these verses how near you are at home. A few more days of labor and sorrow, and the King of kings shall send for you; and in a moment your warfare shall be at end, and all shall be peace.

VII. Faith's Choice

"By faith Moses, when he was come to years, refused to be called the son of Pharaoh's daughter; choosing rather to suffer affliction with the people of god, than to enjoy the pleasures of sin for a season; esteeming the reproach of Christ greater riches than the treasures in Egypt: for he had respect unto the recompense of the reward."

HEBREWS XI. 24-26.

THE eleventh chapter of the Epistle to the Hebrews is a great chapter, I need not tell you. I can well believe it must have been most cheering and encouraging to a converted Jew. I suppose none found so much difficulty in a profession of Christianity as the Hebrews did. The way was narrow to all, but preeminently so to them. The cross was heavy to all, but surely they had to carry double weight. And this chapter would refresh them like a cordial,—it would be as "wine to those of a heavy heart." Its words would be pleasant as the honey-comb, "sweet to the soul and health to the bones."

The three verses I am going to explain are far from being the least interesting in the chapter. Indeed I think few, if any, have so strong a claim on our attention. And I will tell you why I say so.

It seems to me that the work of faith here spoken of, comes home more especially to our own case. The men of God who are named in the former part of the chapter are all examples to us, beyond question. But we cannot literally do what most of them did, however much we may drink into their spirit. We are not called upon to offer a literal sacrifice like Abel,—or build a literal ark like Noah,—or leave our country literally, and dwell in tents, and offer up our Isaac like Abraham. But the faith of Moses comes nearer to us. It seems to operate in a way more familiar to our own experience. It made him take up a line of conduct such as we must often take up ourselves in the present day, each in our own walk of life. And for this reason I think these three verses deserve more than ordinary consideration.

Now I have nothing but the simplest things to say about them. I shall only try to enforce upon you the greatness of the things that Moses did, and the principle on which he did them. And then perhaps you will be better prepared for the practical instructions which the verses appear to hold out to every one who will receive it.

May the Holy Ghost bless the subject to us all! May He give us the same spirit of faith, that we may walk in the steps of Moses, do as he did, and share his reward!

I. First then I will speak of *what Moses gave up and refused*.

Moses gave up three things for the sake of his soul. He felt that his soul would not be saved if he kept them,—so he gave them up. And in so doing I say that he made three of the greatest sacrifices that man's heart can make.

1. *He gave up rank and greatness.*

"He refused to be called the son of Pharaoh's daughter." You all know his history. The daughter of Pharaoh had preserved his life, when he was an infant,—adopted him and educated him as her own son.

If writers of history may be trusted, she was Pharaoh's only child. Men go so far as to say that in the common order of things Moses would one day have been king of Egypt. That may be, or may not—we cannot tell. It is enough for us to know that, from his connection with Pharaoh's daughter, Moses might have been, if he had pleased, a very great man. If he had been content with the position in which he found himself at the Egyptian court, he might easily have been among the first, — if not the very first, — in all the land of Egypt.

Think, Reader, for a moment, how great this temptation was.

Here was a man of like passions with ourselves. He might have had as much greatness as earth can well give. Rank, power, place, honor, titles, dignities, — all were before him, and within his grasp. These are the things for which many men are continually struggling. These are the prizes which there is such an incessant race in the world around us to obtain. To be somebody, — to be looked up to, — to raise themselves in the scale of society, — to get a handle to their names; — these are the things for which many sacrifice time, and thought, and health, and life itself. But Moses would not have them at a gift. He turned his back upon them. He refused them. He gave them up.

2. And more than this, *he refused pleasure*.

Pleasure of every kind, no doubt, was at his feet, if he had liked to take it up, — sensual pleasure, intellectual pleasure, — social pleasure, — whatever could strike his fancy. Egypt was a land of artists, — a residence of learned men, — a resort of every one who had skill, or science of any description. There was nothing which could feed the lust of the flesh, the lust of the eye, or the pride of life, which one in the place of Moses might not easily have commanded.

Think again, Reader, how great was this temptation also.

This, be it remembered, is the one thing for which millions live. They differ perhaps in their views of what makes up real pleasure, — but all agree in seeking first and foremost to obtain it. Pleasure and enjoyment in the holidays is the grand object to which a school-boy looks forward. Pleasure and satisfaction in making himself independent, is the mark on which the young man in business fixes his eye. Pleasure and ease in retiring from business with a fortune, is the aim which the merchant sets before him. Pleasure and bodily comfort at his own house is the sum of the poor man's wishes. Pleasure and fresh excitement in politics, in travelling, in amusements, in company, in books,—this is the goal towards which the rich man is straining. Pleasure is the shadow that all alike are hunting,—high and low,—rich and poor,—old and young, one with another; each perhaps pretending to despise his neighbor for seeking it,—each in his own way seeking it for himself,—each secretly wondering that he does not find it,—each firmly persuaded that somewhere or other it is to be found. This was the cup that Moses had before his lips. He might have drank as deeply as he liked of earthly pleasure. But he would not have it. He turned his back upon it. He refused it. He gave it up.

3. And more than this, *he refused riches*.

"The Treasures in Egypt" is an expression that seems to tell of wealth that he might have enjoyed, had he been content to remain with Pharaoh's daughter. We may well suppose these treasures would have been a mighty fortune. Enough is still remaining in Egypt to give us some faint idea of the money at its' king's disposal. The pyramids, and obelisks, and statues, are still standing there as witnesses. The ruins at Carnac, and Luxor, and Denderah, and many other places, are still the mightiest buildings in the world. They testify to this day that the man who gave up Egyptian wealth, gave up something which even our English minds would find it hard to reckon up.

Think once more, how great was this temptation.

Consider, Reader, the power of money,—the immense influence that the love of money obtains over men's minds. Look around you and see how men covet it, and what amazing pains and trouble they will go through to obtain it. Tell them of an island many thousand miles away, where something may be found which may be profitable if imported, and at once a fleet of ships will be sent to get it. Show them a way to make one per cent, more of their money, and they will reckon you among the wisest of men,—they will almost fall down and worship you. To possess money seems to hide defects,—to cover over faults,—to clothe a man with virtues. People can get over much, if you are rich. But here is a man who might have been rich, and would not. He would not have Egyptian treasures. He turned his back upon them. He refused them. He gave them up.

Such were the things that Moses refused,—rank, pleasure, riches, all three at once.

Add to all this that he did it *deliberately*. He did not refuse these things in a hasty fit of youthful excitement.—He was forty years old. He was in the prime of life. He knew what he was about. He weighed both sides of the question.

Add to it that he did not refuse them *because he was obliged*. He was not like the dying man, who tells us, "He craves nothing more in this world;" and why?—Because he is leaving the world, and cannot keep it. He was not like the pauper, who makes a merit of necessity, and says, "He does not want riches;" and why?—Because he cannot get them. He was not like the old man, who boasts "that he has laid aside worldly pleasures;" and why?—Because he is worn out, and cannot enjoy them. No! Reader. Moses refused what he might have kept, and gave up what he might have enjoyed. Rank, pleasure, and riches did not leave him, but he left them.

And then judge whether I am not right in saying that his was one of the greatest sacrifices mortal man ever made. Others have refused much, but none, I think, so much as Moses, Others have done well in the way of self-sacrifice and self-denial, but he excels them all.

II. And now let me go on to the second thing I wish to set before you. I will speak of *what Moses chose*.

I think his choice as wonderful as his refusal. He chose three things for his soul's sake. The road to salvation led through them, and he followed it; and in so doing he chose three of the last things that man is ever disposed to take up.

1. For one thing *he chose suffering and affliction*.

He left the ease and comfort of Pharaoh's court, and openly took part with the children of Israel. They were an enslaved and persecuted people,—an object of distrust, suspicion, and hatred; and the man who befriended them was sure to taste something of the bitter cup they were daily drinking.

To man's eye there seemed no chance of their deliverance from bondage, without a long and doubtful struggle. A settled home and country for them must have appeared a thing never likely to be obtained, however much desired. In fact, if ever man seemed to be choosing pain, trials, poverty, want, distress, anxiety, perhaps even death, with his eyes open, Moses was that man.

Think only, Reader, how wonderful was this choice.

Man naturally shrinks from pain. It is in us all to do so. We draw back by a kind of instinct from suffering, and avoid it if we can. If two courses of action are set before us, which both seem right, we always take that which is the least disagreeable to flesh and blood. We spend our days in fear and anxiety, when we think affliction is coming near us, and use every means to escape it. And when it does come, we often fret and murmur under the burden of it; and if we can but bear it patiently we count it a great matter indeed.

But look here. Here is a man of like passions with yourself, and he actually chooses affliction!

Moses saw the cup of suffering that was before him if he left Pharaoh's court, and he chose it, preferred it, and took it up.

2. But he did more than this, *he chose the company of a despised people*.

He left the society of the great and wise, among whom he had been brought up, and joined himself to the children of Israel. He who had lived from infancy in the midst of rank, and riches, and luxury, came down from his high estate, and cast in his lot with poor men, — slaves, bondservants, oppressed, destitute, afflicted, tormented, — laborers in the brick-kiln.

How wonderful, once more, was this choice!

Generally speaking we think it enough to carry our own troubles. We may be sorry for others whose lot is to be mean and despised, — we may even try to help them, — we may give money to raise them, — we may speak for them to those on whom they depend; but here we generally stop.

But here is a man who does far more. He not merely feels for despised Israel, but actually goes down to them, adds himself to their society, and lives with them altogether. You would wonder if some great man in Grosvenor or Belgrave Square were to give up house, and fortune, and position in society, and go to live on a small allowance in some narrow lane in Bethnal Green, for the sake of doing good: — yet this would convey a very faint and feeble notion of the kind of thing that Moses did. He saw a despised people, and he chose their company in preference to that of the noblest in the land. He became one with them, — their fellow, their associate, and their friend.

3. But he did even more. *He chose reproach and scorn*.

Who can conceive the torrent of mockery and ridicule that Moses would have to stem, in turning away from Pharaoh's court to join Israel?

Men would tell him he was mad, foolish weak, silly, out of his mind; he would lose his influence; he would forfeit the favor and good opinion of all among whom he had lived.

Think again, Reader, what a choice this was!

There are few things more powerful than ridicule and scorn. It can do far more than open enmity and persecution. Many a man who would march up to a cannon's mouth, or lead a forlorn hope, or storm a breach, has found it impossible to face the mockery of a few companions, and has flinched from the path of duty to avoid it. To be laughed at! To be made a joke of! To be jested and sneered at! To be reckoned weak and silly! To be thought a fool!—There is nothing grand in all this, and many cannot make up their minds to undergo it.

Yet there is a man who made up his mind to it, and did not shrink from the trial. Moses saw reproach and scorn before him, and he chose them, and accepted them for his portion.

Such then were the things that Moses chose,—affliction,—the company of a despised people,—and scorn.

Set down beside all this, that Moses was no weak, ignorant, illiterate person, who did not know what he was about. You are specially told he was a "learned" man,—he was one "mighty in words and in deeds," and yet he chose as he did.

Set down too the circumstances of His choice. He was not obliged to choose as he did. None compelled him to take such a course. The things he took up did not force themselves upon him against his will. He went after them,—they did not come after him. All that he did, he did of his own free choice,—voluntarily, and of his own accord.

And then judge whether it is not true, that his choice was as wonderful as his refusal. Since the world began, I suppose, none ever made such a choice as the man Moses did in our text.

III. And now let me go on to a third thing:—*let me speak of the principle which moved Moses, and made him do as he did.*

How can this conduct of his be accounted for? What possible reason can be given for it? To refuse that which is generally called a good,—to choose that which is commonly thought an evil,—this is not the way of flesh and blood,—this is not the manner of man,—this requires some explanation. What will that explanation be?

You hear the answer in the text. I know not whether its greatness or its simplicity is more to be admired. It all lies in one little word, and that word is, "FAITH."

Moses had faith. Faith was the mainspring of his wonderful conduct. Faith made him do as he did, choose what he chose, and refuse what he refused. He did it all because he believed.

God set before the eyes of his mind His own will and purpose. God revealed to him that a Saviour was to be born of the stock of Israel,—that mighty promises were bound up in these children of Abraham, and yet to be fulfilled,—that the time for fulfilling a portion of these promises was at hand,—and Moses put credit in this, and believed. And every step in his wonderful career,—every action in his journey through life, after leaving Pharaoh's court,—his choice of seeming evil, his refusal of seeming good,—all must be traced up to this fountain, all will be found to rest on this foundation,—God had spoken to him, and he had faith in God's word.

He believed that God would *keep His promises*; that what He had said He would surely do; and what He had covenanted He would surely perform.

He believed that with God *nothing was impossible*. Reason and sense might say that the deliverance of Israel was out of the question,—the obstacles were too many, the difficulties too great. But faith told Moses that God was all-sufficient. God had undertaken the work, and it would be done.

He believed that God was *all wise*. Reason and sense might tell him that his line of action was absurd;—he was throwing away useful influence and destroying all chance of benefiting his people, by breaking with Pharaoh's daughter. But faith told Moses that if God said, "Go this way," it must be the best.

He believed that God was *all merciful*. Reason and sense might hint that a more pleasant manner of deliverance might be found; that some compromise might be effected, and many hardships be avoided. But faith told Moses that God was love, and would not give His people one drop of bitterness beyond what was absolutely needed.

Faith was a *telescope* to Moses. It made him see the godly land afar off,—rest, peace, victory,—when dim-sighted reason could only see trial and barrenness, storm and tempest, weariness and pain.

Faith was an *interpreter* to Moses. It made him pick out a comfortable meaning in the dark commands of God's handwriting, while ignorant sense could see nothing in it all but mystery and foolishness.

Faith told Moses that all this rank and greatness was of the earth, earthy; a poor, vain, empty thing, frail, fleeting, and passing away; and that there was no true greatness like that of serving God. He was the king, he the true nobleman who belonged to the family of God. It was better to be last in heaven, than first in hell.

Faith told Moses that worldly pleasures were pleasures of sin. They were mingled with sin,—they led on to sin,—they were ruinous to the soul, and displeasing to God. It would be small comfort to have pleasure while God was against him. Better suffer and obey God, than be at ease and sin.

Faith told Moses that these pleasures after all were only for a season:—they could not last,—they were all short-lived,—they would weary him soon,—he must leave them all in a few years.

Faith told him there was a reward in heaven for the believer, far richer than the treasures in Egypt;—durable riches, where rust could not corrupt, nor thieves break through and steal. The crown there would be incorruptible;—the weight of glory would be exceeding and eternal;—and faith bade him look away to that if his eyes were dazzled with Egyptian gold.

Faith told Moses that affliction and suffering were not real evils:—they were the school of God, in which he trains the children of grace for glory;—the medicines which are needful to purify our corrupt wills;—the furnace which must burn away our dross;—the knife which must cut loose the ties that bind us to the world.

Faith told Moses that this despised people were the people of God; that to them belonged the adoption, and covenant, and the promises, and the glory; that of them the seed of the woman was one day to be born, who should bruise the serpent's head; that the special blessing of God was upon them; that they were lovely and beautiful in His eyes;—and that it was better to be a door-keeper among the people of God, than to reign in the palaces of wickedness.

Faith told Moses that all the reproach and scorn poured out on him was the reproach of Christ;—that it was honorable to be mocked and despised for Christ's sake;—that whoso persecuted Christ's people was persecuting Christ Himself;—and that the day must come when His enemies would bow before Him and lick the dust.

All this, and much more, of which I cannot speak particularly, Moses saw by faith. These were the things he believed, and believing did what he did. He was persuaded of them, and embraced them,—he reckoned them as certainties,—he regarded them as substantial verities,—he counted them as sure as if he had seen them with his eyes,—he acted on them as realities,—and this made him the man that he was.

Marvel not that he refused greatness, riches, and pleasure.—He looked far forward. He saw with the eye of faith kingdoms crumbling into dust,—riches making to themselves wings and fleeing away,—pleasures leading on to death and judgment,—and Christ only and His little flock enduring forever.

Wonder not that he chose affliction, a despised people, and reproach.—He beheld things below the surface. He saw with the eye of faith affliction lasting but for a moment,—reproach rolled away, and ending in everlasting honor,—and the despised people of God reigning as kings with Christ in glory.

And, Reader, was he not right? Does he not speak to us, though dead, this very day? The name of Pharaoh's daughter has perished;—the city where Pharaoh reigned is not known;—the treasures in Egypt are gone:—but the name of Moses is known wherever the Bible is read, and is still a standing witness that whoso liveth by faith, happy is he.

IV. And now let me wind up all by trying to set before you some *practical lessons, which appear to me to follow from this text*.

What has all this to do with us? some men will say. We do not live in Egypt,—we have seen no miracles,—we are not Israelites,—we are weary of the subject.

Stay a little, Reader, if this be the thought of your heart, and by God's help I will show you that all may learn here, and all may be instructed.

1. For one thing, *if ever you would be saved, you must make the choice that Moses made,—you must prefer God before the world*.

Reader, mark well what I say. Do not overlook this, though all the rest be forgotten. I do not say that the statesman must throw up his office, and the rich man forsake his property. Let no one fancy that I mean this. But I say, if a man would be saved, whatever be his rank in life, he must be prepared for tribulation; he must make up his mind to choose that which seems evil, and to give up and refuse that which seems good.

I dare be sure this sounds strange language to some who read these pages. I know well you may have a certain form of religion, and find no trouble in your way. There is a common worldly kind of Christianity in this day, which many have, and think they have enough,—a cheap Christianity which offends nobody, and requires no sacrifice,—which costs nothing, and is worth nothing. I am not speaking of religion of this kind.

But if you really are in earnest about your soul,—if your religion is something more than a mere fashionable cloak,—if you are determined to live by the Bible,—if you are resolved to be a New Testament Christian, then, I repeat, you will soon find you must carry a cross,—you must endure hard things,—you must suffer because of your soul, as Moses did, or you cannot be saved.

The world in the nineteenth century is what it always was. The hearts of men are still the same. The offence of the cross is not ceased. God's true people are still a despised little flock. True evangelical religion still brings with it reproach and scorn. A real servant of God will still be thought by many a weak enthusiast and a fool.

Reader, do you wish your souls to be saved? Then remember, you must choose whom you will serve. You cannot serve God and mammon. You cannot be on two sides at once. You cannot be a friend of Christ, and a friend of the world at the same time. You must come out from the children of this world, and be separate; you must put up with much ridicule, trouble, and opposition, or you are lost forever. You must be willing to think and do things which the world considers foolish, and to hold opinions which are only held by a few. It will cost you something. The stream is strong, and you have to stem it. The way is narrow and steep, and it is no use saying it is not. But depend on it, there can be no saving religion without sacrifices and self-denial.

Now, Reader, are you doing anything of this kind? I put it to your conscience in all affection and tenderness, are you, like Moses, preferring God to the world, or not? I beseech you not to take shelter under that dangerous word "we,"—"we ought,"—and "we hope,"—and "we mean,"—and the like. I ask you plainly, what are you doing yourself? Are you willing to give up anything which keeps you back from God? or are you clinging to the Egypt of the world, and saying to yourself, "I must have it, I must have it, I cannot tear myself away?" What sacrifices are you making? Are you making any at all? Is there any cross in your Christianity? Are there any sharp corners in your religion, anything that ever jars and comes in collision with the earthly-mindedness around you, or is all smooth and rounded off, and comfortably fitted in to custom and fashion? Do you know anything of the afflictions of the Gospel? Is your faith and practice ever a subject of scorn and reproach? Are you thought a fool by any one because of your soul? Have you left Pharaoh's daughter, and heartily joined the people of God? Are you venturing all on Christ? Search and see.

Reader, these are hard and rough sayings.—I cannot help it.—I believe they are founded on Scripture truths. I remember it is written, "there were great multitudes with Jesus, and he turned and said unto them, If any man come unto me and hate not his father, and mother, and wife, and children, and brethren, and sisters, yea and his own life also, he cannot be my disciple. And whosoever doth not bear his cross, and come after me, cannot be my disciple." (Luke xiv. 25, 27.) Many, I fear, would like glory, who have no wish for grace,—they would fain have the wages, but not the work,—the harvest, but not the labor,—the reaping, but not the sowing,—the reward, but not the battle. But it may not be. As Bunyan says, "the bitter must go before the sweet." If there is no cross there will be no crown.

2. The second thing I will say is this,—*nothing will ever enable you to choose God before the world, except faith.*

Nothing else will do it. Knowledge will not;—feeling will not;—a regular use of outward forms will not;—good companions will not. All these may do something, but the fruit they produce has no power of continuance, it will not last. A religion springing from such sources will only endure so long as there is no tribulation or persecution because of the word; but so soon as there is any, it will dry up. It is a clock without weights,—its face may be beautiful, you may turn its fingers round, but it will not go.

A religion that is to stand must have a living foundation, and there is none other but faith.

Reader, have you got this faith? If you have, you will find it possible to refuse seeming good, and choose seeming evil,—you will think nothing of to-day's losses, in the hope of to-morrow's gains,—you will follow Christ in the dark, and stand by Him to the very last. If you have not, I warn you, you will never war a good warfare, and so run as to obtain,—you will soon be offended and turn back to the world.

There must be a real belief that God's promises are sure and to be depended on;—a real belief that what God says in the Bible is all true, and that every doctrine contrary to this is false, whoever may say it. There must be a real belief that all God's words are to be received, however hard and disagreeable to flesh and blood, and that his way is right, and all others wrong; this there must be, or you will never come out from the world, take up the cross, follow Christ, and be saved.

You must learn to believe promises better than possession;—things unseen better than things seen;—things in heaven out of sight, better than things on earth before your eyes;—the praise of the invisible God better than the praise of visible man. Then, and then only, you will make a choice like Moses, and prefer God to the world.

This was the faith by which the old saints obtained a good report. This was the weapon by which they overcame the world. This made them what they were.

This was the faith that made Noah go on building his ark, while the world looked on and mocked,—and Abraham gave the choice of the land to Lot, and dwell on quietly in tents,—and Ruth cleave to Naomi, and turn away from her country and her gods,—and Daniel continue in prayer, though he knew the lions' den was prepared,—and the three children refuse to worship idols, though the fiery furnace was before their eyes. All these acted as they did because they believed. Well may the Apostle Peter speak of faith as "precious faith." (2 Peter i. 1.)

3. The third thing I shall say is this, *the true reason why so many are worldly and ungodly persons is, that they have no faith*.

Reader, you must be aware that multitudes of professing Christians would never think for a moment of doing as Moses did. It is useless to speak smooth things, and shut our eyes to the fact. That man must be blind who does not see thousands around him who are daily preferring the world to God,—placing the things of time before the things of eternity,—the things of the body before the things of the soul. You may not like to hear it, but so it is.

And why do they do so? No doubt they will all give us reasons and excuses. Some will talk of the snares of the world,—some of the want of time,—some of the peculiar difficulties of their position,—some of the cares and anxieties of life,—some of the strength of temptation,—some of the power of passions,—some of the effects of bad companions. But what does it come to after all? There is a far shorter way to account for the state of their souls, *they do not believe*. One simple sentence, like Aaron's rod, will swallow up all their excuses, *they have no faith*.

They do not really think what God says is true. They secretly flatter themselves with the notion, "it will surely not be fulfilled, all of it;—there must surely be some other way to heaven besides that which ministers speak of; there cannot surely be so much danger of being lost." In short they do not put implicit confidence in the words that God has written and spoken, and so do not act upon them. They do not thoroughly believe hell, and so do not flee from it;—nor heaven, and so do not seek it;—nor the guilt of sin, and so do not turn from it;—nor the holiness of God, and so do not fear Him;—nor their need of Christ, and so do not trust in Him, nor love Him. They do not feel confidence in God, and so venture nothing for Him. Like the boy Passion, in Pilgrim's Progress, they must have their good things now. They do not trust God, and so they cannot wait.

Reader, how is it with yourself? Do you believe all the Bible? Ask yourself that question. Depend on it, it is a much greater thing to believe all the Bible than many suppose. Happy is the man who can say, "I am *a believer*."

We talk of infidels sometimes as if they were the rarest people in the world. And I grant you that open avowed infidelity is happily not common now. But there is a vast amount of practical infidelity around us, for all that, which is as dangerous in the end as the principles of Voltaire and Paine. There are many who Sunday after Sunday repeat their creed, and make a point of declaring their belief in all that the Apostolic and Nicene forms contain, and yet these very persons will live all the week as if Christ had never died? and as if there were no judgment, and no resurrection of the dead, and no life everlasting at all. There are many who will say, "Oh, we know it all," when spoken to about eternal things, and the value of their souls; and yet their lives show plainly they know not anything as they ought to know; and the saddest part of their state is, that they think they do.

Reader, I warn you that knowledge not acted upon, in God's sight, is no knowledge at all. A faith that does not influence a man's practice is not worthy of the name. There are only two classes in the Church of Christ,—those who believe, and those who do not. The difference between the true Christian and the mere outward professor, just lies in one word;—the true Christian is like Moses, "he has faith;"—the professor has none. The true Christian believes, and therefore lives as he does;—the mere professor does not believe, and therefore is what he is. Oh! where is your faith! Be not faithless, but believing.

4. The last thing I will say is this, *the true secret of doing great things for God is, to have great faith.*

I suspect that we are all apt to err a little on this point. We think too much, and talk too much about graces, and gifts, and attainments, and do not sufficiently remember that faith is the root and mother of them all. In walking with God, a man will go just as far as he believes, and no further. His life will always be proportioned to his faith. His peace, his patience, his courage, his zeal, his works,—all will be according to his faith.

You read the lives of eminent Christians perhaps. Such men as Romaine, or Newton, or Martyn, Scott, or Simeon, or M'Cheyne; and you are disposed to say, "What wonderful gifts and grace these men had!" I answer, you should rather give honor to the mother-grace which God puts forward in the eleventh chapter of the

Epistle to the Hebrews,—you should give honor to their faith. Depend on it, faith was the mainspring in the character of each and all.

I can fancy some one saying, "They were so prayerful;—that made them what they were." I answer, why did they pray much?—Simply because they had much faith. What is prayer, but faith speaking to God?

Another perhaps will say, "They were so diligent and laborious,—that accounts for their success." I answer, why were they so diligent?—Simply because they had faith. What is Christian diligence, but faith at work?

Another will tell me, "They were so bold,—that rendered them so useful." I answer, why were they so bold?—Simply because they had much faith. What is Christian boldness, but faith honestly doing its duty?

And another will cry, "It was their holiness and spirituality,—that gave them their weight." For the last time I answer, what made them holy?—Nothing but a living, realizing spirit of faith. What is holiness, but faith visible and faith incarnate?

Now, dear Reader, would you grow in grace, and in the knowledge of our Lord Jesus Christ? Would you bring forth much fruit? Would you be eminently useful? Would you be bright, and shine as a light in your day? Would you, like Moses, make it clear as noon-day that you have chosen God before the world? I dare be sure that every believer will reply, "Yes! yes! yes! these are the things we long for and desire."

Then take the advice I give you this day:—go and cry to the Lord Jesus Christ, as the disciples did, "Lord, increase our faith." Faith is the root of a real Christian's character. Let your root be right, and your fruit will soon abound. Your spiritual prosperity will always be according to your faith. He that believeth shall not only be saved, but shall never thirst,—shall overcome,—shall be established,—shall walk firmly on the waters of this world,—and shall do great works.

VIII. REMEMBER LOT

"He lingered."
GENESIS XIX. 16.

WHO is this man that lingered?—Lot, the nephew of faithful Abraham. And when did he linger?—The very morning when Sodom was to be destroyed. And where did he linger?—Within the walls of Sodom itself. And before whom did he linger?—Under the eyes of the two angels, who were sent to bring him out of the city.

Reader, the words are solemn, and full of food for thought. I trust they will make you think. Who knows but they are the very words your soul requires? The voice of the Lord Jesus commands you to "remember Lot's wife." (Luke xvii. 32.) The voice of one of His ministers invites you this day to remember Lot.

Let me try to show you,—

I. *What Lot was himself*:

II. *What the text already quoted tells you of him*:

III. *What reasons may account for his lingering*:

IV. *What kind of fruit his lingering brought forth.*

I. *What was Lot?*

This is a most important point. If I leave it unnoticed, I shall perhaps miss that class of professing Christians I want especially to benefit. You would perhaps say, after reading this paper, "Ah! Lot was a poor, dark creature,—an unconverted man,—a child of this world;—no wonder he lingered."

But mark now what I say. Lot was nothing of the kind. Lot was a true believer,—a real child of God,—a justified soul,—a righteous man.

Has any one of you grace in his heart?—So also had Lot.

Has any one of you a hope of salvation?—So also had Lot.

Is any one of you a new creature?—So also was Lot.

Is any one of you a traveller in the narrow way which leads unto life?—So also was Lot.

Do not think this is only my private opinion, a mere arbitrary fancy of my own,—a notion unsupported by Scripture. Do not suppose I want you to believe it, merely because I say it. The Holy Ghost has placed the matter beyond controversy, by calling him "just," and "righteous," (2 Peter ii. 7, 8,) and has given us evidence of the grace that was in him.

One evidence is, that he lived in a wicked place, "seeing and hearing" evil all around him, (2 Peter ii. 8,) and yet was not wicked himself. Now to be a Daniel in Babylon, an Obadiah in Ahab's house, an Abijah in Jeroboam's family, a saint in Nero's court, and a righteous man in Sodom, a man must have the grace of God.

Another evidence is, that he "vexed his soul with the unlawful deeds" he beheld around him. (2 Peter ii. 8.) He was wounded, grieved, pained, and hurt at the sight of sin. This was feeling like holy David, who says, "I beheld the transgressors, and was grieved, because they kept not thy word." "Rivers of waters run down mine eyes, because they keep not thy law." (Psalm cxix. 136, 158.) Nothing will account for this but the grace of God.

Another evidence is, that he "vexed his soul from day to day" with the unlawful deeds he saw. (2 Peter ii. 8.) He did not at length become cool and lukewarm about sin, as many do. Familiarity and habit did not take off the fine edge of his feelings, as too often is the case. Many a man is shocked and startled at the first sight of wickedness, and yet becomes at last so accustomed to see it, that he views it with comparative unconcern. This is especially the case with those who live in great cities. But it was not so with Lot. And this is a great mark of the reality of his grace.

Such an one was Lot,—a just and righteous man, a man sealed and stamped as an heir of heaven by the Holy Ghost Himself.

Reader, before you pass on, remember that a true Christian may have many a blemish, many a defect, many an infirmity, and yet be a true Christian nevertheless. You do not despise gold because it is mixed with much dross. You must not undervalue grace because it is accompanied by much corruption. Read on, and you will find that Lot paid dearly for his lingering. But do not forget, as you read, that Lot was a child of God.

II. Let us pass on to the second thing I spoke of. *What does the text, already quoted, tell us about Lot's behavior?*

The words are wonderful and astounding, "He lingered;" and the more you consider the time and circumstances, the more wonderful you will think them.

Lot knew the awful condition of the city in which he stood; "the cry" of its abomination "had waxen great before the Lord:" (Gen. xix. 13,) and yet he lingered.

Lot knew the fearful judgment coming down on all within its walls; the angels had said plainly, "The Lord hath sent us to destroy it:" (Gen. xix. 13,) and yet he lingered.

Lot knew that God was a God who always kept His word, and if He said a thing would surely do it. He could hardly be Abraham's nephew, and live long with him, and not be aware of this. Yet he lingered.

Lot believed there was danger, for he went to his sons-in-law, and warned them to flee: "Up," he said, "get you out of this place; for the Lord will destroy this city." (Gen. xix. 14.) And yet he lingered.

Lot saw the angels of God standing by, waiting for him and his family to go forth. And yet he lingered.

Lot heard the voice of those ministers of wrath ringing in his ears to hasten him, "Arise lest thou be consumed in the iniquity of the city." (Gen. xix. 15.) And yet he lingered.

He was slow when he should have been quick—backward when he should have been forward—trifling when he should have been hastening—loitering when he should have been hurrying—cold when he should have been hot. It is passing strange! It seems almost incredible! It appears too wonderful to be true! But the Spirit writes it down for our learning. And so it was.

And yet, Reader, there are many of the Lord Jesus Christ's people very like Lot.

Mark well what I say. I repeat it, that there may be no mistake about my meaning. I have shown you that Lot lingered,—I say that there are many Christian men and Christian women in this day very like Lot.

There are many real children of God, who appear to know far more than they live up to, and see far more than they practise, and yet continue in this state for many years. Wonderful that they go as far as they do, and yet go no further!

They hold the Head, even Christ, and love the truth. They like sound preaching, and assent to every article of Gospel doctrine, when they hear it. But still there is an indescribable *something* which is not satisfactory about them. They are constantly doing things which disappoint the expectations of their ministers, and of more advanced Christian friends. Marvellous that they should think as they do, and yet stand still!

They believe in heaven, and yet seem faintly to long for it;—and in hell, and yet seem little to fear it. They love the Lord Jesus, but the work they do for Him is small. They hate the devil, but they often appear to tempt him to come to them. They know the time is short, but they live as if it were long. They know they have a battle to fight, yet a man might think they were at peace. They know they have a race to run, yet they often look like people sitting still. They know the judge is at the door, and there is wrath to come, and yet they appear half asleep. Astonishing they should be what they are, and yet be nothing more!

And what shall we say of these people? They often puzzle godly friends and relations. They often cause great anxiety. They often give rise to great doubts and searchings of heart. But they may be classed under one sweeping description: they are all brethren and sisters of Lot. *They linger*.

These are they who get the notion into their minds that it is impossible for all believers to be very holy and very spiritual. They allow that eminent holiness is a beautiful thing. They like to read about it in books, and even to see it occasionally in others. But they do not think that all are meant to aim at so high a standard. At any rate they seem to make up their minds it is beyond their reach.

These are they who get into their heads false ideas of *charity*, as they call it. They would fain please everybody, and suit everybody, and be agreeable to everybody. But they forget they ought first to be sure that they please God.

These are they who dread sacrifices, and shrink from self-denial. They never appear able to apply our Lord's command, "to cut off the right hand and pluck out the right eye." (Matt. v. 29, 30.) They spend their lives in trying to make the gate more wide, and the cross more light. But they never succeed.

These are they who are always trying to keep in with the world. They are ingenious in discovering reasons for not separating decidedly, and in framing plausible excuses for attending questionable amusements, and keeping up questionable friendships. One day you are told of their attending a Bible reading: the next day perhaps you hear of their going to a ball. They are constantly laboring to persuade themselves that to mix *a little* with worldly people on their own ground does good. Yet in their case it is very clear they do no good, and only get harm.

These are they who cannot find it in their heart to quarrel with their besetting sin, whether it be sloth, indolence, ill-temper, pride, selfishness, impatience, or what it may. They allow it to remain a tolerably quiet and undisturbed tenant of their hearts. They say it is their health, and their constitutions, and their temperaments, and their trials, and their way. Their father, or mother, or grandmother, was so before themselves, and they are sure they cannot help it. And when you meet after the absence of a year or so, you hear the same thing.

But all, all, all may be summed up in one single sentence. They are the brethren and sisters of Lot. *They linger*.

Ah! render, if you are a lingering soul, you are not happy. You know you are not. It would be strange indeed if you were so. Lingering is the sure destruction of a happy Christianity. A lingerer's conscience forbids him to enjoy inward peace.

Perhaps at one time you did run well. But you have left your first love,—you have never felt the same comfort since, and you never will till you return to your first works. Like Peter, when the Lord Jesus was taken prisoner, you are following the Lord afar off, and like him you will find the way not pleasant but hard.

Come and look at Lot. Come and mark Lot's history. Come and consider Lot's lingering, and be wise.

III. Let us next consider *the reasons that may account for Lot's lingering*.

This is a question of great importance, and I ask your serious attention to it. To know the root of a disease is one step towards a remedy. He that is forewarned is forearmed.

Who is there among the readers of these pages that feels secure, and has no fear of lingering? Come and listen while I tell you a few passages in Lot's history. Do as he did, and it will be a miracle indeed if you do not get into the same state of soul at last.

One thing, then, I observe in Lot, is this, *he made a wrong choice in early life*.

There was a time when Abraham and Lot lived together. They both became rich, and could live together no longer. Abraham, the elder of the two, in the true spirit of humility and courtesy, gave Lot the choice of the country, when they resolved to part company; "If thou," he said, "wilt take the left hand then I will go to the right, or if thou depart to the right hand then I will go to the left." (Gen. xiii. 9.)

And what did Lot do? — We are told he saw the plains of Jordan, near Sodom, were rich, fertile and well-watered. It was a good land for cattle, and full of pastures. He had large flocks and herds, and it just suited his requirements. And this was the land he chose for a residence, simply because it was a rich, well-watered land.

It was near the town of Sodom! He cared not for that.

The men of Sodom, who would be his neighbors, were wicked! It mattered not.

They were sinners before God exceedingly! It made no difference to him.

The pasture was rich. The land was good. He wanted such a country for his flocks and herds. And before that argument all scruples and doubts, if indeed he had any, at once went down.

He chose by sight, and not by faith. He asked no counsel of God to preserve him from mistakes. He looked to the things of time, and not of eternity. He thought of his worldly profit, and not of his soul. He considered only what would help him in this life,—he forgot the solemn business of the life to come. This was a bad beginning.

But I observe also that *Lot mixed with sinners when there was no occasion for his doing so.*

We are first told that he "pitched his tent toward Sodom." (Gen. xiii. 12.) This, as I have already shown, was a great mistake.

But the next time he is mentioned, we find him actually living in Sodom itself. The Spirit says expressly, "He dwelt in Sodom." (Gen. xiv. 12.) His tents were left. The country was forsaken. He occupied a house in the very streets of that wicked town.

We are not told the reasons of this change. We are not aware that any occasion could have arisen for it. We are sure there could have been no command of God. Perhaps his wife liked the town better than the country, for the sake of society. It is plain she had no grace herself. Perhaps she persuaded Lot it was needful for the education of his daughters. Perhaps the daughters urged living in the town for the sake of gay company: they were evidently light-minded young women. Perhaps Lot liked it himself, in order to make more of his flocks and herds. Men never want reasons to confirm their wills. But one thing is very clear,—Lot dwelt in the midst of Sodom without good cause.

Reader, when a child of God does these two things, which I have named, you never need be surprised if you hear, by-and-by, unfavorable accounts about his soul. You never need wonder if he becomes deaf to the warning voice of affliction, as Lot was, (Gen. xiv. 12.) and turns out a lingerer in the day of trial and danger, as Lot did.

Make a wrong choice,—an unscriptural choice,—in life, and settle yourself down unnecessarily in the midst of worldly people, and I know no surer way to damage your own spirituality, and to go backward about your eternal concerns.

This is the way to make the pulse of your soul beat feebly and languidly. This is the way to make the edge of your feeling about sin become blunt and dull. This is the way to dim the eyes of your spiritual discernment, till you can scarcely distinguish good from evil, and stumble as you walk. This is the way to bring a moral palsy on your feet and limbs, and make you go tottering and trembling along the road to Zion, as if the grasshopper was a burden.

This is the way to sell the pass to your worst enemy,—to give the devil the vantage-ground in the battle,—to tie your arms in fighting,—to fetter your legs in running,—to dry up the sources of your strength,—to cripple your own energies,—to cut off your own hair, like Samson, and give yourself into the hands of the Philistines, put out your own eyes, grind at the mill, and become a slave.

Reader, wake up and mark well what I am saying. Settle these things down in your mind. Do not forget them. Recollect them in the morning. Recall them to memory at night. Let them sink down deeply into your heart. If ever you would be safe from lingering, beware of needless mingling with worldly people. Beware of Lot's choice. If you would not settle down into a dry, dull, sleepy, idle, barren, heavy, carnal, stupid, torpid state of soul, *beware of Lot's choice*.

Remember this in choosing a dwelling-place or residence. It is not enough that the house is comfortable,—the situation good,—the air fine,—the neighborhood pleasant,—the expenses small,—the living cheap. There are other things yet to be considered. You must think of your immortal soul. Will the house you think of help you towards heaven or hell?—Is the Gospel preached within easy distance?—Is Christ crucified within reach of your door?—Is there a real man of God near, who will watch over your soul? I charge you, if you love life, not to overlook this. *Beware of Lot's choice*.

Remember this in choosing a calling, a place, or profession in life. It is not enough that the salary is high, the wages good,—the labor light, the advantages numerous,—the prospects of getting on most favorable. Think of your soul, your immortal soul. Will it be fed or starved? Will it be prospered or drawn back? I beseech you, by the mercies of God, to take heed what you do. Make no rash decision. Look at the place in every light, the light of God as well as the light of the world. Gold may be bought too dear. *Beware of Lot's choice*.

Remember this in choosing a husband or wife, if you are unmarried. It is not enough that your eye is pleased,—that your tastes are met,—that your minds find congeniality,—that there is amiability and affection,—that there is a comfortable home for life. There needs something more than this. There is a life yet to come. Think of your soul, your immortal soul Will it be helped upwards, or dragged downwards by the union you are planning?—Will it be made more heavenly, or more earthly,—drawn nearer to Christ, or to the world?—Will its religion grow in vigor, or will it decay? I pray you, by all your hopes of glory, allow this to enter into your calculations. Think, as old Baxter said, and think, and think, and think again, before you commit yourself. "Be not unequally yoked." (2 Cor. vi. 14.) Matrimony is nowhere named among the means of conversion. *Remember Lot's choice*.

Remember this, if you are ever offered a situation on a railway. It is not enough to have good pay, and regular employment, the confidence of the directors, and the best chance of rising to a higher post. These things are very well in their way, but they are not everything. How will your soul fare, if you serve a railway company that runs Sunday trains?—What day in the week will you have for God and eternity?—What opportunities will you have for hearing the Gospel preached? I solemnly warn you to consider this. It will profit you nothing to fill your purse, if you bring leanness and poverty on your soul. Beware of selling your Sabbath for the sake of a good place. *Beware of Lot's choice*.

Reader, you may perhaps think, "a believer need not fear,—he is a sheep of Christ,—he will never perish,—he cannot come to much harm. It cannot be that such small matters can be of great importance."

Well! you may think so; but I warn you, if you neglect them, your soul will never prosper. A true believer will certainly not be cast away, although he may linger; but if he does linger, it is vain to suppose his religion will thrive.

Grace is a tender plant. Unless you cherish it, and nurse it well, it will soon become sickly in this evil world. It may droop, though it cannot die. The brightest gold will soon become dim, when exposed to a damp atmosphere. The hottest iron will soon become cold. It requires pains and toil to bring it to a red heat. It requires nothing but letting alone, or a little cold water, to become black and hard.

You may be an earnest, zealous Christian now. You may feel like David in his prosperity, "I shall never be moved." (Psalm xxx. 6.) But be not deceived. You have only got to walk in Lot's steps, and make Lot's choice, and you will soon come to Lot's state of soul. Allow yourself to do as he did,—presume to act as he acted, and be very sure you will soon discover you have become a wretched lingerer, like him.

You will find like Samson, the presence of the Lord is no longer with you. You will prove, to your own shame, an undecided, hesitating man, in the day of trial. There will come a canker on your religion, and eat out its vitality without your knowing it. There will come a consumption on your spiritual strength, and waste it away insensibly. And at length you will wake up to find your hands hardly able to do the Lord's work, and your feet hardly able to carry you along the Lord's way, and your faith no bigger than a grain of mustard-seed;—and this perhaps at some turning point in your life, at a time when the enemy is coming in like a flood, and your need is the sorest.

Ah! Reader, if you would not become a lingerer in religion, consider these things. Beware of doing what Lot did.

IV. Let us inquire now *what kind of fruit Lot's lingering spirit bore at length*.

I would not pass over this point for many reasons, and especially in the present day.

There are not a few who will feel disposed to say, "After all Lot was saved,—he was justified,—he got to heaven. I want no more. If I do but get to heaven I shall be content."

Reader, if this be the thought of your heart, just stay a moment and listen to me a little longer. I will show you one or two things in Lot's history, which deserve attention, and may perhaps induce you to alter your mind.

I think it of first importance to dwell upon this subject. I always will contend that eminent holiness and eminent usefulness are most closely connected,—that happiness and following the Lord fully go side by side,—and that if believers will linger, they must not expect to be useful in their day and generation, or to enjoy great comfort and peace in believing.

Mark then, for one thing, *Lot did no good among the inhabitants of Sodom*.

Lot lived in Sodom many years. No doubt he had many precious opportunities for speaking of the things of God, and trying to turn away souls from sin. But Lot seems to have effected just nothing at all. He appears to have had no weight or influence with the people who lived around him. He possessed none of that respect and reverence which even the men of the world will frequently concede to a bright servant of God.

Not one righteous person could be found in all Sodom, outside the walls of Lot's home. Not one of his neighbors believed his testimony. Not one of his acquaintances honored the Lord when he worshipped. Not one of his servants served his master's God. Not one of "all the people from every quarter" cared a jot for his opinion when he tried to restrain their wickedness. "This one fellow came into sojourn," said they, "and he will needs be a judge." (Gen. xix. 9.) His life carried no weight. His words were not listened to. His religion drew none.

And truly I do not wonder. As a general rule, lingering souls do no good to the world, and bring no credit to God's cause. Their salt has too little savor to season the corruption around them. They are not epistles of Christ, that can be known and read of all. (2 Cor. iii. 2.) There is nothing magnetic, and attractive, and Christ-reflecting about their ways. Remember this.

Mark another thing. *Lot helped no relation towards heaven*.

We are not told how large his family was. But this we know,—he had a wife and two daughters at least, in the day he was called out of Sodom, if he had not more children besides.

But whether Lot's family was large or small, one thing, I think, is perfectly clear,—there was not one among them all that feared God.

When he "went out and spake to his sons-in-law which married his daughters," and warned them to flee from the coming judgments, we are told, "he seemed to them as one that mocked." (Gen. xix. 14.) What fearful words those are! It was as good as saying, "Who cares for anything *you* say?" So long as the world stands those words will be a painful proof of the contempt with which a lingerer in religion is regarded.

And what was Lot's wife? She left the city in his company, but she did not go far. She had not faith to see the need of such a speedy flight. She left her heart in Sodom when she began to flee. She looked back from behind her husband, in spite of the plainest commands not to do so, (Gen. xix. 17,) and was at once turned into a pillar of salt.

And what were Lot's two daughters? They escaped indeed, — but only to do the devil's work. They became their father's tempters to wickedness, and led him to commit the foulest of sins.

In short, Lot stood alone in his family. He was not made the means of keeping one soul back from the gates of hell.

And I do not wonder. Lingering souls are seen through by their own families, and when seen through despised. Their nearest relations understand inconsistency if they understand nothing else in religion. They draw the sad, but not unnatural conclusion, "Surely if he believed all he professes to believe, he would not go on as he does." Lingering parents seldom have godly children. The eye of the child drinks in far more than the ear. A child will always observe what you do much more than what you say. Remember this.

Mark a third thing. *Lot left no evidences behind him when he died.*

We know but little about Lot after his flight from Sodom, and all that we do know is unsatisfactory. His pleading for Zoar, because it was "a little" city, — his departure from Zoar afterwards, — and his conduct in the cave, — all, all tell the same story. All show the weakness of the grace that was in him, and the low state of soul into which he had fallen.

We know not how long he lived after his escape. We know not where he died, or when he died, — whether he saw Abraham again, — what was the manner of his death, — what he said, or what he thought. All these are hidden things. We are told of the last moments of Abraham, Isaac, Jacob, Joseph,—but not one word about Lot. Oh! what a gloomy death-bed the death-bed of Lot must have been!

The Scripture appears to draw a veil around him on purpose. There is a painful silence about his latter end. He seems to go out like an expiring lamp, and leave an evil savor behind him. And had we not been specially told in the New Testament that Lot was "just" and "righteous," I verily believe we should have doubted whether Lot was a saved soul at all.

But I do not wonder at his sad end. Lingering believers will generally reap according as they have sown. Their lingering often meets them when their spirit is departing. They have little peace at the last. They reach heaven, to be sure, but they reach it in darkness and storm. They are saved, but saved so as by fire.

Reader, consider these three things I have just mentioned. Do not misunderstand my meaning. It is amazing to observe how readily people catch at the least excuse for misunderstanding the things that concern their souls!

I do not tell you that believers who do not linger will, as a matter of course, be great instruments of usefulness to the world. Noah preached one hundred and twenty years, and none believed him. The Lord Jesus was not esteemed by His own people, the Jews.

Nor yet do I tell you that believers who do not linger will, as a matter of course, be the means of converting their families and relations. David's children were many of them ungodly. The Lord Jesus was not believed even by His own brethren. (John vii. 5.)

But I do say it is almost impossible not to see a connection between Lot's evil choice, and Lot's lingering,—and between Lot's lingering, and his unprofitableness to his family and the world. I believe the Spirit meant us to see it. I believe the Spirit meant to make it a beacon to all professing Christians. And I am sure the lessons I have tried to draw from the whole history, deserve serious reflection.

Let me speak a few parting words to all who read this paper, and especially to all who call themselves believers in Christ.

I have no wish to make your hearts sad. I do not want to give you a gloomy view of the Christian course. My only object is to give you friendly warnings. I desire your peace and comfort. I would fain see you happy, as well as safe,—and joyful as well as justified. I speak, as I have done, for your good.

You live in days when a lingering, Lot-like religion abounds. The stream of profession is far broader than it once was, but far less deep in many places. A certain kind of Christianity is almost fashionable now. To belong to some party in the church, and show a zeal for its interests,—to talk about the leading controversies of the day,—to buy popular religious books as fast as they come out, and lay them on your table,—to attend meetings,—subscribe to societies,—and discuss the merits of preachers,—all these are now comparatively easy and common attainments. They no longer make a person singular. They require little or no sacrifice. They entail no cross.

But to walk closely with God,—to be really spiritually-minded,—to behave like strangers and pilgrims,—to be distinct from the world in employment of time, in conversation, in amusements, in dress,—to bear a faithful witness for Christ in all places,—to leave a savor of our Master in every society,—to be prayerful, humble, unselfish, meek,—to be jealously afraid of sin, and tremblingly alive to our danger from the world,— these, these are still rare things. They are not common among those who are called true Christians, and worst of all, the absence of them is not felt and bewailed as it should be.

Reader, I give you good counsel this day. Do not turn from it. Do not be angry with me for plain speaking. I bid you give diligence to make your calling and election sure. I bid you not to be slothful,—not to be careless,—not to be content with a small measure of grace,—not to be satisfied with being a little better than the world. I solemnly warn you not to attempt doing what never can be done,—I mean to serve Christ, and yet keep in with the world. I call upon you, and beseech you, I charge you, and exhort you,—by all your hopes of heaven, and desires of glory,—*do not be a lingering soul*.

Would you know what the times demand,—the shaking of nations,—the uprooting of ancient things,—the overturning of kingdoms,—the stir and restlessness of men's minds? They all say,—*Christian! do not linger!*

Would you be found ready for Christ at His second appearing,—your loins girded,—your lamp burning,—yourself bold and prepared to meet Him? *Then do not linger!*

Would you enjoy much sensible comfort in your religion,—feel the witness of the Spirit within you,—know in whom you have believed,—and not be a gloomy and melancholy Christian? *Then do not linger!*

Would you enjoy strong assurance of your own salvation in the day of sickness, and on the bed of death?—Would you see with the eye of faith heaven opening, and Jesus rising to receive you? *Then do not linger!*

Would you leave great broad evidences behind you, when you are gone?—Would you like us to lay you in the grave with comfortable hope, and talk of your state after death without a doubt? *Then do not linger!*

Would you be useful to the world in your day and generation?—Would you draw men from sin to Christ, and make your Master's cause beautiful in their eyes? *Then do not linger!*

Would you help your children and relations towards heaven, and make them say, "We will go with you?" and not make them infidels and despisers of all religion? *Then do not linger!*

Would you have a great crown in the day of Christ's appearing, and not be the least and smallest star in glory, and not find yourself the last and lowest in the kingdom of God? *Then do not linger!*

Oh! let none of us linger. Time does not,—death does not,—judgment does not,—the devil does not,—the world does not. Neither let the children of God linger.

Reader, are you a lingerer? Has your heart felt heavy, and your conscience sore, while you have been reading these pages? Does something within you whisper, "I am the man?" Reader, listen to what I am saying,—how is it with your soul?

If you are a lingerer, you must just go to Christ at once and be cured,—you must use the old remedy. You must bathe in the old fountain. You must turn again to Christ, and be healed. The way to do a thing is to do it. Do this at once.

Think not for a moment your case is past recovery. Think not because you have been long living in a dry and heavy state of soul, that there is no hope of revival. Is not the Lord Jesus Christ an appointed Physician for the soul? Did He not cure every form of disease? Did not He cast out every kind of devil? Did He not raise poor backsliding Peter, and put a new song in his mouth? Oh! doubt not, but earnestly believe that He will yet revive His work within you. Only turn from lingering, and confess your folly, and come,—come at once to Christ. Blessed are the words of the prophet, "Only acknowledge thine iniquity,"—"Return, ye backsliding children, and I will heal your backsliding." (Jerem. iii. 13, 22.)

Reader, remember the souls of others, as well as your own. If at any time you see any brother or sister lingering, try to awaken them,—try to arouse them,—try to stir them up. Let us all exhort one another as we have opportunity. Let us provoke unto love and good works. Let us not be afraid to say to each other, "Brother, or sister, have you forgotten Lot? Awake! and remember Lot!—Awake and linger no more."

www.ingramcontent.com/pod-product-compliance
Lightning Source LLC
Chambersburg PA
CBHW011315080526
44587CB00024B/4003